The Seventeenth Highland Light Infantry (Glasgow Chamber of Commerce Battalion)

17TH H.L.I.
THE GIFT OF THE MEMBERS OF THE GLASGOW CHAMBER
OF COMMERCE

The Seventeenth Highland Light Infantry (Glasgow Chamber of Commerce Battalion)

During the First World War
1914-1918

John W. Arthur

Ion S. Munro

LEONAUR

The Seventeenth Highland Light Infantry
(Glasgow Chamber of Commerce Battalion)
During the First World War
1914-1918
by John W. Arthur
Ion S. Munro

First published under the title
The Seventeenth Highland Light Infantry.
(Glasgow Chamber of Commerce Battalion)

Leonaur is an imprint
of Oakpast Ltd

ISBN: 978-0-85706-306-9 (hardcover)
ISBN: 978-0-85706-305-2 (softcover)

http://www.leonaur.com

Publisher's Notes

Contents

Part 3.—An Odd Muster

Part 4.—Honours and Awards

Original Editors' Preface

In compiling and editing this history of the Chamber of Commerce Battalion, the aim of the editors has been to present such a narrative as will provide a detailed but not overburdened account of the Battalion's movements and operations throughout the years of its existence, and at the same time give a representative impression of the various outstanding events which have built up the character and the traditions of the unit.

In accordance with the wishes of the History Committee, the narrative dealing with Field service has been kept within the limits of the Battalion's share in the campaign, and accordingly no attempt has been made to give any picture of the relative positions of the various other units operating with the 17th, or of the general strategic import of the actions described.

The chapters dealing with the beginnings and home training, and those general items in Part 3 are founded mainly upon matter supplied by officers of the unit and members of *The Outpost* staff. The Roll of original members in Part 4 has been gathered together by Lieut. and Quarter-Master Kelly. The material in the section dealing with the service of the Battalion overseas has been gathered from the following sources:—

For data—the Official War Diaries of the 17th Battalion H.L.I. preserved in the "Records" Office, Hamilton; supplementary notes supplied by Lieut.-Cols. Morton and Paul and Major Paterson, D.S.O., M.C.; Brigade and Battalion Operation Orders; Battalion Operation Reports.

For impressions, opinions, and descriptions—numerous and exceedingly helpful literary vignettes from members of *The Outpost* staff and others, and from interviews.

The Editors desire to record their appreciation of material contributed and help given by:—Lieut.-Col. Morton, Lieut.-Col. Paul, Lieut.-Col. Inglis, Major Paterson, the Rev. A. Herbert Gray, C.F., Capt. G.H.R. Laird, Capt. M. MacRobert, Capt. T.P. Locking, Mr. Cameron of the Chamber of Commerce, Lieut. and Quarter-Master Kelly, Mr. Meadows of Saltcoats (for allowing illustrations and excerpts to be taken from the diary of his son, the late Lieut. B. Meadows), the relatives of the late Lieut. D.W. Hourston (for a selection of photographs from his collection), and the following gentlemen identified with the publication of *The Outpost*:—Messrs. A.M. Cohen, W.S. Corbett, Mark Drummond, W.M. Dixon, A.G. Deans, W. Glennie, A.G. Houstoun, J.L. Hardie, C. MacCallum, J. M'Kechnie, N. M'Intyre, W.K. M'Taggart, D. Murray, J.L.L. Niven, F.K. Pickles, H.F. Scott, D.M. Thomson, R. Tilley.

John W. Arthur.
Ion S. Munro.
Glasgow, May, 1920.

THEY ASK A BETTER BRITAIN AS THEIR MONUMENT.

1.—FORMATION AND HOME TRAINING

The Nation's Call to Arms

Great Britain declared war on Germany on August 4th, 1914, and almost immediately the combatant strength of its Regular Army was on service and the great bulk of that gallant force engaged in those fierce actions against odds which marked the early fighting.

The War Office was quickly alive to the fact that the Regular Army could not cope in point of numbers with the Germanic hordes. On the day following the declaration of war the Territorial Forces of Great Britain were mobilized, and with a marvellous and inspiring unanimity their members volunteered for Overseas Service. But even the addition of these many thousands to our striking force was realised to provide no more than a relief for the rapidly exhausting strength of the "old contemptibles," and Lord Kitchener issued his great manifesto calling the people to the Empire's help, and laid the foundations of a New Army—Kitchener's Army—the finest and most disinterested body of soldier patriots that ever stepped in a sound and worthy cause.

At once the patriotism of the country declared itself and the Nation sprang to arms. The City of Glasgow proved itself second to none among the cities and districts of the Kingdom in its answer to the call. The Town Council recruited two fine battalions, the 1st Glasgow, which was mainly drawn from the Tramway employees of the city; and the 2nd Glasgow, which was recruited from former members of the Boys' Brigade. Other institutions in the city were bestirring themselves in the national cause, and at a meeting of the Chamber of Commerce Directors, held on 3rd September, 1914, it was unanimously resolved, on the motion of Bailie W.F. Russell, to form a Glasgow Chamber of Commerce Battalion. Enthusiasm for the scheme was quickly evident, and no time was lost in getting the matter put upon a practical basis.

At the same meeting of Directors the following gentlemen were appointed as the Committee in charge:—Messrs. M.M.W. Baird, James W. Murray, F.C. Gardiner, G.A. Mitchell, H. Moncrieff, W.F. Russell, A.A. Smith, with Sir Archd. M'Innes Shaw as Convener, and Mr. John W. Arthur as Vice-Convener, the former making Military matters his chief concern, the latter caring for Clothing and Equipment. Mr. Montagu M.W. Baird, the President, and Mr. James W. Murray, the Vice-President, did much to foster the movement.

The Chamber of Commerce sustained the loss of Mr. Baird, who died on October 14, 1915. Mr. J.W. Murray succeeded him as President and applied that deep interest in all the work and welfare of the Battalion which marked his services throughout the history of the unit. Mr. Thomas Cameron, the Secretary of the Chamber, also in countless ways contributed to its success.

At this stage the Council of the Royal Glasgow Technical College approached the Chamber of Commerce Committee, and it was arranged that students of the College would find special opportunities of forming a detachment within the Battalion. This arrangement was found acceptable in every way, and many students entered for the service of their country under the colours of what was at that early stage known as "The Chamber of Commerce Battalion, 3rd Glasgow."

THE LATE MR. MONTAGU M.W. BAIRD,
PRESIDENT OF THE CHAMBER,
1914–1915.

MR. JAMES W. MURRAY,
PRESIDENT OF THE CHAMBER,
1916–1917–1918.

A Battalion in Being

No time was lost in bridging the gap between "Resolution" and "Action." By September 12th, 1914, the work of enrolling recruits had begun, and Medical Examination and Attestation were commenced under the supervision of Colonel J. Stanley Paterson, Officer in Charge, No. 2 District, Scottish Command. Colonel Paterson did much for the Battalion in many directions, and in a recent letter says:—"

"I have never lost, and never will lose, the deep interest I took in the 17th H.L.I. from the moment of its initiation, and the full story of its doings will give me the greatest pleasure to read."

The Lesser Hall of the Merchants' House was for many days the Headquarters of busy recruiting, and those associated with these stirring times will long remember the enthusiasm with which the enrolment was conducted. With the help of Dr. Beilby and Mr. Stockdale of the Royal Technical College, "A" Company was speedily recruited, and was composed mainly of the College Students. Colonel R.C. Mackenzie, C.B., did much for "B" Company, enlisting in its ranks former pupils of the City Schools, the High School, Glasgow Academy and others. "C" and "D" Companies were composed principally of men from the business houses and different trades in the city and district. For a few weeks the men, living in their own homes, were instructed and drilled in four of the Territorial Force Association Halls. During the recruiting and the early weeks of the training, Major Rounsfell Brown acted as Adjutant, and rendered excellent service.

Kit was issued to the four original Companies, "A," "B," "C," and "D," on 19th and 20th September.

It was at first expected that Colonel Fred. J. Smith, late of the 8th Scottish Rifles, might be chosen as Officer in Command, but for reasons of health he was unable to undertake the duty. The choice eventually fell upon Lieut.-Colonel David S. Morton, V.D., who had seen much service, and was well fitted to fill the post. His volunteer experience included service in the 1st L.R.V., the Engineers, and various Commissioned ranks in the 5th H.L.I., ending, on his retiral, with the rank of Lieut.-Colonel. In 1900 he served with the 71st in South Africa as Captain of the H.L.I. Service Company. He was mentioned in despatches, and received the "South Africa" Medal with three clasps.

Major W.J. Paul was appointed second in Command. His service had been with the Scottish Rifles (the 4th V.B.S.R.), in which unit he rose to the rank of Major, second in Command. He retired in 1907 with the Honorary rank of Major.

The original officers in command of companies were:—

"A" Major W.J. Paul.
"B" Major J.R. Young.
"C" Major W. Auld, V.D.
"D" Major E. Hutchison.

The Regimental Staff included Captain D.R. Kilpatrick, R.A.M.C., as Surgeon attached; Lieut. and Quarter-Master Slade; Regimental Sergt.-Major Kelly; Regimental Quarter-Master Sergt. T. Keith; and Orderly Room Quarter-Master-Sergt. J. Copland.

Up to this point the drill and training were being well pushed on. It will be remembered that the extraordinary demands made on khaki cloth, by the sudden institution of a national army, made it practically unobtainable in these early months. A navy blue serge cloth was substituted for making tunics, trousers and greatcoats, and these made a neat and serviceable uniform. This uniform was issued at Gailes and was exchanged for khaki in the following summer at Troon.

The Battalion was now ready to set out for its war training station, and on 23rd September assembled in the Examination Hall of the Royal Technical College, and had a good send-off by the directors and members of the Chamber of Commerce, Colonel Stanley Paterson, and other friends. At this meeting, colours for the Regiment were promised by Mr. Montagu M.W. Baird, the President of the Chamber; bugles, by Dr. and Mrs. Beilby, of the Technical College; and pipes and drums as a joint gift by the directors of the Chamber of Commerce and Merchants' House. After the meeting, the Battalion entrained for the camp at Gailes.

A member of the Battalion, giving a general impression of these memorable "first days," writes:—

MAJOR W.J. PAUL.

MAJOR JOHN R. YOUNG.

MAJOR W. AULD, V.D.

MAJOR E. HUTCHISON.

The Farewell Meeting in the Technical College.

We all assembled in our various drill halls. We watched and whispered. Some asked, who is that man with the loud voice shouting at us, giving us papers and getting us into what he called Companies. We knew soon. Then they selected N.C.O.'s (acting) from amongst those who had some previous training. After that we went away. The N.C.O.'s stayed and took the bundles of papers, our pledged word to our king, and wearily for hours sorted them and listed the names.

Days followed when we marched and when we got to know our officers by sight and to call ourselves by our Company name. Then came the day we drew our kit and carried off strange bundles to our homes. We got the magic words 'To camp at Gailes.' Then we were soldiers now. We paraded by Companies and assembled in the Square and marched to the train. A motley crowd carrying on our shoulders all manner of weird shaped bundles. The crowd laughed and cheered us. Thus we left the City that held us very peculiarly her own, her citizens and sons for the last time. Henceforth her soldiers.

The Chamber of Commerce Battalion was now an accomplished fact, and the following authoritative acceptance by the Government and the War Office, linked it as an integral part of the Service Regiments of the British Army.

War Office,
London, S.W., 2nd November, 1914.

To The President,
    Chamber of Commerce,
        7 West George Street,
            Glasgow.

Sir,

I am commanded by the Army Council to offer you, and those associated with you, their sincere thanks for having raised the 17th (Service) Battalion, Highland Light Infantry (3rd Glasgow) of which the administration has now been taken over by the Military Authorities.

The Council much appreciated the spirit which prompted your offer of assistance, and they are gratified at the successful results of the time and labour devoted to this object, which has added to the armed forces of the Crown the services of a fine body of men.

The Council will watch the future career of the Battalion with interest, and they feel assured that when sent to the front it will maintain the high reputation of the distinguished Regiment of which it forms part.

I am to add that its success on active service will largely depend on the result of your efforts to keep the depot Companies constantly up to establishment with men in every way fit for service in the field.

I am, Sir,

Your obedient Servant,

(Signed)   B.B. Cubitt.

On 7th November, the Battalion paid a return visit to the city of Glasgow. The Battalion arrived and formed up on the station platform. A word of command and away they marched into the streets, crowded to the uttermost by friends and relatives. Hardly a cheer was heard. The men marched between banks of faces, in a deep silence. What a strange reception, surely the most impressive men ever had, proving what was in the hearts of those that watched the men and how they felt for them. Only when they entered the Square did cheers and the buzzing of an awaking crowd break out. "We felt," says an officer, "rather disappointed; but we knew what it meant." The unit was then inspected in front of the Municipal Buildings by representatives of the Chamber of Commerce.

EARLY DAYS.

A REST BY THE WAY.

H.R.H. The Duke of Connaught,
Colonel-in-Chief of the H.L.I.

Colonel J. Stanley Paterson.

Esprit de Corps

It will be of value and interest to give here a brief survey of the history of The Highland Light Infantry, which enshrines a record of service and gallantry second to none in the annals of our Empire, and to which the Chamber of Commerce Battalion was fated to add a page as heroic and imperishable as any in its great traditions.

The Highland Light Infantry was originally raised as two separate Regiments of Foot, the 71st and the 74th. What was to become famous as the 71st was raised in 1777 by Lord John MacLeod and was known as "MacLeod's Highlanders." It was a kilted regiment and wore the Mackenzie tartan. It was originally numbered the 73rd, and under this designation won early distinctions in India in the campaigns against Hyder Ali and Tippoo Sahib. Nine years after its inauguration it became the 71st, and after service in Ceylon and at the Cape it received in 1808 the title of "The Glasgow Regiment." Shortly after this the 71st entered once more the fields of war in the Peninsula campaign under Wellington, and shared in many actions including the storming of Ciudad Rodrigo, the siege of Badajoz and at Vittoria. Then came their crowning gallantry at Waterloo against the flower of Napoleon's armies. In later years the Crimea, Canada and the Bermudas were added to their war honours.

The 74th was raised at Glasgow by Major-General Sir Archibald Campbell with a view to service in India. The 74th also wore the kilt, but of Black Watch tartan. Their record runs much on the same lines as that of the 71st, and quickly they are also found performing deeds of stubborn gallantry in India in the Mysore Territory. When the hour of Tippoo Sahib had come, the 74th was the first to enter the tyrant's last stronghold, but it was later, at the battle of Assaye that they earned a fame which finds its echo today in the old badge of the Elephant, which that action entitles them to wear. For long afterwards the unit possessed the proud by-name of "The Assaye Regiment." After sharing with the 71st in the rigours of the Peninsula, Canada and the West Indies, the 74th saw service in the Kaffir War, Madras, and in Egypt, including Tel-el-Kebir, where they were in the fiercest of the fight.

It was in 1809, as a reward for their services, that they were formed into Light Infantry, and were permitted to retain such parts of the national dress as were not inconsistent with the duties of Light Infantry. They then discarded the kilt and adopted the tartan trews which still appear in the full dress uniform of the Regiment. The kilt is now worn by two Territorial Battalions, the 6th and the 9th.

Subsequently the two regiments were formed into one regiment of two battalions.

The "H.L.I.," as all the world calls it, was of course present during the South African War. They fought at Modder River, and though they suffered severely at Magersfontein, continued to share in the hardships of the remainder of the campaign.

At the outbreak of the Great War there were in addition to the 1st and 2nd Battalions, two Special Reserve Battalions (the 3rd and 4th) and five Territorial Battalions, numbered the 5th, 6th, 7th, 8th and 9th.

After declaration of war, the 10th, 11th, 12th, 13th, 14th, 15th, 16th, 17th, 18th, 19th and 20th Service Battalions were raised, together with the 21st (Territorial) and 1st (Garrison) Battalions. In addition, the 5th, 6th, 7th, 8th and 9th Battalions each had second and third lines, and at one time there were as many as thirty Battalions in existence. These were more or less connected with the City of Glasgow and district, and serve as an indication of the patriotism and loyalty of the community.

On 14th December, 1914, the War Office issued an order that the Chamber of Commerce Battalion was to form a unit of the New Army, and was to be designated the 17th (Service) Battalion Highland Light Infantry, of the 117th Infantry Brigade, of the 39th Division. This intimation was received when the Battalion was stationed at Troon, and was hailed with great enthusiasm by all ranks.

Their comradeship in the common cause, their keenness for practical service and the *esprit de corps* engendered by their attachment to the illustrious Highland Light Infantry, knit all ranks together in enthusiasm and determination.

It was about this time that instructions were received to recruit a fifth Company as part of the 17th Battalion establishment. As this

On the Sea Front at Troon.

Lt.-Col. David S. Morton,
V.D., C.M.G.

Leaving Troon.

"Guard, Turn Out"—Wensley Camp

Mess Orderlies—Prees Heath Camp.

Company eventually became the nucleus of a further Battalion with a parallel history of its own, it will be treated separately in another chapter. (Part 3, "E" Company.)

Home Stations and Training

The Battalion arrived at Gailes on 23rd September, 1914, and this event might be called the beginning of the Great Adventure. The war seemed miles nearer as the light-hearted and high-spirited lads stepped out of the train and viewed the rows of glistening white tents. The large array of kit bags was in many instances supplemented by suit cases, filled with surplus personal effects thought necessary for creature comforts. The novelty of the surroundings, and twelve men in a tent, including numerous belongings, did not conduce to sleep; and the next morning *reveillé* found all but the old soldier already astir. The weeks at Gailes were spent in organising, and the efforts of all ranks to become efficient were worthy of that spirit which lasted throughout the existence of the Battalion.

The issue of something in the nature of a uniform and a few Drill Pattern rifles raised hopes that the training was being hurried on. On the 13th October, a move was made to Troon, where the good citizens afforded luxurious billets to the Battalion.

In spite of the vigorous training that was enforced during the next few months, and which stood the men in such good stead later on, the social side was not neglected and helped to cement a great feeling of good fellowship and understanding between the officers and men. It was with mutual regret that the Seventeenth took its departure from Troon on 13th May, 1915, and the memory of the stay in the Ayrshire town will always remain as one of the most pleasant memories in the history of the Battalion.

There is something very remarkable about the record of the 17th H.L.I. when billeted in Troon. For though brain-weary subalterns spent hours trying to balance their billeting monies to the satisfaction of exasperated and exacting Company Commanders, there was very little trouble in the Orderly Room, that pulse of trouble.

Here are some noteworthy facts:—

1.—The Guard Room was always empty.

2.—There were practically no men "crimed" for lateness on parade.

3.—There were practically no "crimes" for being out of "billets."

4.—There were no complaints of rowdyism in billets.

5.—There were no charges of drunkenness.

6.—There were only very few charges of pass breaking.

7.—There were very few claims for damage, and these on examination were more vindictive than real.

8.—It was not necessary to serve any billeting notices.

These are a few of the significant facts that mount up to bring honour to the rank and file of the 17th H.L.I.

The three troop-trains carrying the Battalion arrived at Whitchurch, Shropshire, on the morning of the 14th May, and the men marched some three miles south to the great hut-city on Prees Heath. This was the first War Station of the Brigade, where the 15th, 16th and 17th H.L.I. joined the 11th (S.) Battalion Border Regiment (The Lonsdales).

There the men found hut life very comfortable. The cleaning and tidying of their new abodes kept them busy, and was carried out with the cheery zest and whole-hearted enthusiasm so characteristic of the Seventeenth. Full advantage was taken of the adjacent Y.M.C.A. establishment, which proved an admirable Institution. The concert hall, refreshment tables, reading and billiard rooms, were well patronised at all off-duty hours, and the men appreciated the cheerful kindness of the attendants, who were voluntary lady workers from the County houses.

Extended manoeuvres were impracticable in this well-fenced agricultural area, so the training embraced much route-marching, and barrack-square work, musketry, signalling, visual training, etc. There were several trying marches in the scorching May-June weather, to Clive's native district, Moreton-Say and Market Drayton, to Wem and Hodnet, and to the beautiful scenery of Hawkstone Park, and Iscoyd Hall. Football, cricket, hockey, golf and cross-country running provided healthy recreation, while excursions to old-world "Sleepy Chester," to Shrewsbury and into Wales were popular weekends.

In the third week of June, 1915, the 17th H.L.I. changed quarters

A Peaceful Bivouac—Salisbury Plain.

Recruiting March at Codford.

from the flat stifling district of Prees-Heath to the breezy upland valley of Wensleydale, in the North Riding of Yorkshire. There is hardly a level acre in the district, but this was a welcome change. Many an enjoyable journey was made, in the intervals of Brigade Training, northward to lonely Swaledale, south to Coverdale, across the Valley of the Yore, to the prominent peak of Penhill, or to the beautiful Aysgarth Falls.

The Infantry Brigade, the 97th, had the 95th and the South Irish Horse as comrades for the training round Leyburn and Middleham, and Bellerby Moors; and some pleasant friendships were formed with the Warwickshire and Gloucestershire lads, and with the "foine foightin' bhoys" from Cork and Tipperary.

On the 27th of July tents were shifted to Totley Rifle Ranges in Derbyshire, where the preliminary Musketry Course was fired by the Battalion during the next fortnight, with most creditable results. The men made themselves great favourites in Totley and Dore, and at Sheffield, where they received a very hospitable welcome at all times, and especially on the occasion of a memorable route march through that city on 9th August. The Battalion was given an enthusiastic send-off at Dore and Beauchief Stations on 10th August, when entraining for Salisbury Plain, the scene of their next training ground.

When the Seventeenth steamed into the station at Codford St. Mary, on 11th August, and saw the occasional houses peeping through the tall trees, it was the thought that, after the bustle and stir of Totley, they had indeed become soldiers in earnest. The Camp Warden strengthened this belief with his assurance that no unit stayed longer than six weeks in the camp, and after that,—Southampton and France, for the testing and proof of all that had been learnt so eagerly. As it turned out, three months were spent at Codford—months of rigorous training, of long interesting divisional manoeuvres, and general hardening.

The men learned to dig trenches quickly and well, for they had to spend nights in them; to march many miles without complaint, and fight at the end of the hardest day's march; to use Lewis guns, not as amateurs with a strange toy, but as men whose lives depended on their speed and ability. The mysteries of transport, and the value of a timetable were revealed.

Needless to say these days of field exercises were not lacking in some amusing incidents which seem to dog the footsteps of peace conditions manoeuvres and which act as very welcome episodes amid the hard work that such training involves. Towards the close of one of the periodical manoeuvres carried out by the Seventeenth under the critical eye of an Inspecting General a bugle had sounded and the manoeuvres ceased. Officers grouped together and men lay on their backs and talked. The general turned to one of the Battalion officers who were now beginning to assemble round him, and said, "What was that call?" He often did such things as this to test knowledge of detail.

"The Stand Fast," said the officer to whom the question was addressed.

"Oh! come! come!" said the general, "Now, what was it?" he further questioned a company commander. No reply came. Then he turned to the second in command, "Now, Major, what was it? Tell him."

"The Stand Fast, sir," said the major.

"Really," said the general, "you gentlemen must learn the elementary things in soldiering. Bugler, tell these gentlemen what that call was."

"The Stand Fast, sir," replied the bugler. The general hurried on with the conference!

At Codford the Battalion had its first taste of army biscuit and bully-beef. From Monday to Thursday manoeuvres were held; on Friday, "clean up," and on Saturday, after the colonel's inspection, the luckier ones went to Bath and Bristol for the day, or to London or Bournemouth for the week-end. Friday was pay day—"Seven Shillings me lucky lad," and after pay-out, the reading of the Army Act or a lecture on bayonet-fighting or tactics. Games flourished. The Battalion football team played and defeated Bath City, and met the other battalions of the division at rugby football, and invariably won. On the ranges with rifle and Lewis gun, the Battalion maintained its place as *the* Battalion in the division.

At last word was received that the Battalion would cross to France on November 22nd. Only fifty per cent. got week-end leave—there was no time for more. Training was over. Few will forget the brave skirl of the pipes as the Battalion swung home in the morning from Yarnbury Castle, file after file silhouetted against the orange and gold of the rising sun. Always, when the wind blows fresh and sweet in the morning, those who are left of those happy times will think of Codford, the "jumping off place" of the Seventeenth for France.

The following message of God-speed and goodwill was received by the Battalion as part of the 32nd Division before setting out:—

Officers of the Battalion at Mar Lodge, Troon, 1915.

Visit of the Directors of the Chamber of Commerce, Troon, 1915.

17th Service Battalion Highland Light Infantry.
Brigade Order No. 1285, of 19th November, 1915.
Message from His Majesty the King.

Officers, Non-Commissioned Officers and Men of the 32nd Division, on the eve of your departure for Active Service I send you my heartfelt good wishes.

It is a bitter disappointment to me, owing to an unfortunate accident, I am unable to see the Division on Parade before it leaves England; but I can assure you that my thoughts are with you all.

Your period of training has been long and arduous, but the time has now come for you to prove on the Field of Battle the results of your instruction.

From the good accounts that I have received of the Division, I am confident that the high traditions of the British Army are safe in your hands, and that with your comrades now in the Field you will maintain the unceasing efforts necessary to bring the War to a victorious ending.

Goodbye and God-speed."

To the above message the following reply was sent:—

Please convey to His Majesty the heartfelt thanks of all ranks of the 32nd Division for His gracious message and their determination to justify His expectations.

The Division deeply regrets the accident which has deprived it of the honour of a visit from His Majesty, and humbly offers its best wishes for His Majesty's speedy and complete recovery.

On Sunday, 21st November, 1915, the Battalion paraded in full strength, 1,032 all ranks, at their hutments, Codford. A minute and final inspection was made, and everything pronounced to be in order. A memorable feature of this parade was the head-gear, Balmoral bonnets of the war service pattern being worn for the first time. Next morning the Battalion left Codford in three parties for Southampton, and without any delay embarked on two transports for Havre, the remainder of the Division going *via* Boulogne. It was a perfect crossing, no wind, bright moonlight, with everyone in the best of spirits.

At 7 a.m. on the 23rd, the troops disembarked at the port of Havre and marched off at once to the Rest Camp, three miles away, great interest being displayed in the few German prisoners working on the docks. On arrival the Battalion found it was under canvas, no floor boards and plenty of mud—a first taste of real discomfort. Moreover the day was raw, with a suspicion of snow, and no one was sorry when it was announced that the camp was being left first thing in the morning. That evening a few of the officers visited the town itself, and others went out on a first reconnaissance to discover the route to the station, and the Ration Depot.

The next day, after drawing two days' rations as well as "Iron Rations," the Battalion left for the "Front,"—"A," "B," and "C" Companies going off at 1.15 p.m., and "D" Company following a few hours later.

Chamber of Commerce Battalion, Troon, April, 1915

2.—Active Service

On Trek

The Battalion arrived at the Port of Le Havre, disembarked in high spirits, and in the morning of 23rd November, 1915, part of the troops left the docks for a three mile trek to a rest camp; but soon the Battalion set out on its first journey "up the line" in cattle trucks. Travelling through the night of the 24th, *via* Rouen and Amiens, the unit reached Pont Remy, some twelve miles east of Abbeville, in the early hours of the following day, and soon had commenced their first route march into the battle-ways of France, and, incidentally, at the first resting place, Mouflers, made cheerily light of what was their first experience of faulty billeting arrangements.

One billet, for 150 men, at the Folie Auberge was uninhabitable, and the appearance of the billets in general was greeted with good-natured growls of amazement and disgust. The weather, however, was mild and sunny, and after about eight hours' work all the troops were more or less under cover. When every incident was an experience novel and suggestive, such minor discomforts did not trouble anyone seriously; but considered in retrospect it must be admitted that these, their first billets, were very poor for a village so far behind the line. If it was an unpromising beginning for the companies, it proved a delusion and a snare for headquarters, for they scored on this occasion in having at the *château* the most comfortable billets they ever were fated to enjoy.

The next day was spent in resting, and on the 27th the march was continued along the magnificent Amiens Road, through Felix-court and Belloy-sur-Somme to La Chaussee. This was a day of keen frost and bright sunshine, and headed by the band, the 17th stepped out through the various villages in the best of spirits. Following the same column was the 17th Northumberland Fusiliers and two A.S.C. Companies. That night the billets were good, everyone felt somehow in holiday mood, helped perhaps by the successful bargaining for eggs, chickens and wine, for to make purchases at all was even at that early date a matter for rejoicing. The pipers delighted with their playing the heart of Madame la Comptesse at her *château* at Turancourt where Brigade headquarters were stationed.

On the 28th, a bitterly cold day, the Battalion marched eleven miles *via* Coisy and Ranneville to Molliens-au-Bois, and there they stayed until the morning of December 1st, when they were joined by M. Duchamps, interpreter. Molliens-au-Bois lies about eight miles north of Amiens, but the outstanding feature was that, from the high ground above there was got the first glimpse of the illuminations provided nightly by the Bosche, all along the battle front.

On 1st December they left at 8.15 a.m., in company with the 16th H.L.I., and on the way a Company of the 17th Northumberland Fusiliers joined the column, which now was moving into the front area.

During the afternoon of that day, the officers and N.C.O.s of "A" and "B" Companies went from Bouzincourt into the front line trenches, just north of Albert, and were attached for instruction to the 7th Gordons and the 7th Black Watch of the 51st Division, and on the following day these two companies joined their officers in the front line for one night. The trenches were in a very bad condition after hard frost and heavy rain. Parts of the trenches were collapsing under the severe conditions and cases were reported from neighbouring units of men being drowned in the mud and water.

On the 3rd and 4th December "C" and "D" Companies from Millencourt went through a similar programme. On the 6th the front line only of Sectors F1 and F2 were taken over, and then on the 8th the whole Battalion took over Sector F1—some 2,000 yards of system from just north of La Boisselle towards Authuille (Blighty) Wood. The front line and communication trenches were knee deep in water and the trench shelters were poor. Rats galore and of enormous size added to the amenity of the district.

On the 4th of December the 17th suffered their first casualty by enemy action, Pte. J.M. Harper, "A" Company, being wounded by a rifle grenade.

The next day Ptes. A. Taylor and R. Cross, of "D" Company, were wounded while bringing up rations. On the afternoon of the 11th, the Battalion, having completed its course of practical instruction, was relieved, and returned, two Companies to Bouzincourt, two to Millencourt. During the relief the enemy shelled the position heavily, and

Havre.

Ruins of Bethune.

the Battalion was fortunate in escaping with only one casualty, Pte. R. M'Kelvie of "B" Company. The next day the Battalion marched back to Molliens-au-Bois, *via* Senlis and Beaucourt, to recuperate after their opening experience of active trench warfare conditions. The mud and water and the dilapidated condition of the trenches were indeed an eye-opener to the men, as much as the comparative absence of "enemy activity." As they tramped back to Molliens, they passed some Companies of the 15th H.L.I. *en route* for their first spell, and their blank astonishment at the muddy appearance of the returning 17th Battalion was much appreciated by the war-worn veterans!

All ranks received a good reception from the villagers, and the next few days were spent in resting, inspections and training. Considerable time was taken up in making duck-boards from the smaller trees of a wood near the village until this exercise was stopped by the forester. A few secured the grant of leave to Amiens, a privilege greatly enjoyed. The work of the organisations home in Glasgow and the interest taken in the Regiment and the men of the 17th Battalion soon became manifested by the arrival of parcels to such an extent that the postal arrangements were severely strained!

Trench Routine

The Battalion returned to the line from Molliens-au-Bois on 23rd December, 1915, and from then till 17th February, 1916, held the Sector F1 alternately with the 11th Border Regiment. The outstanding features of this period were the digging and then the taking over of the new trenches across the big re-entrant on their right on 2nd February, and the enemy raid on the 2nd K.O.Y.L.I., on their left on 9th February.

It will be noted that this spell of trench warfare activities brackets in both Christmas and New Year—both of which were accordingly spent in the front line trenches. As far as possible Christmas fare was provided in the line, and strict orders were issued that if the enemy made any friendly offers they were to be rejected strenuously. The only exchange of greetings notified for Christmas and New Year in the Official War Diary of the Battalion is a brief record of shelling and machine gunning. But during this period the Battalion had nevertheless very few casualties—only seven killed, including two died of wounds. The first casualty was Corporal Houston of No. 16 Platoon, who was killed at Lower Donnet on 3rd January.

Except for patrol work, the piece of work carried out on 2nd February, 1916, in connection with the new trenches was the first military operation carried out by the 17th when in close touch with the enemy, and it was confined to "B" Company and a Platoon of "A" Company, who acted as covering party.

For some time the Battalion had been exercised in night manoeuvres, and on 1st February they had a full-dress rehearsal of the impending operation, which, on Tuesday, 2nd February, came off sooner than had been anticipated. The scheme was to form a new line of trenches, protected by wire, nearer the German line, some 300 yards in front of the existing one, the length dug being about 600 yards, with communication trenches in addition.

At 6 p.m., in pitch darkness, "B" Company filed out into "no man's land." Instructions were, "No firing, bayonet only if necessary." There were Hun flares and machine guns, but no search-light. Had the enemy but used the light, all might have been spoiled. Their lives depended on no Hun reaching their line, or getting back with information. They went straight out the 600 yards without a hitch. That fixed their right flank, where Major J.R. Young was in command. Captain Russell led his half company 500 yards straight across the front, with two scouts on either side, checking.

At every five yards a man dropped and was placed, facing his proper front. They moved slowly, snail pace, but only three times in the 500 yards had the line to drop flat, until the last man was placed. The next thing was to get in touch with "A" Company, who were putting out the platoon to guard "B" Company's left flank. Rather jumpy work, this joining hands in pitch darkness. It was a long, silent night. At 9.30 the tinkling sound of the wire being fixed was heard, and they knew from this that the digging had commenced—some 800 men, good and true, working silently as they had never worked before.

When 1.30 a.m. came their time was up. The right half company, under Major Young, rose silently, and crept off to a place in the wire where a gap had been arranged for the men to pass through. Captain Russell with the left half company followed. The wiring and digging went on till 3 a.m., protected by patrols sent out in front of the wire. A new trench, with communication trenches, had been laid 300 yards out from their old line, protected by treble staked wire, on a frontage of 600 yards. The new trench was held till dawn before handing over. There was no hitch, and not a man wounded.

The Battalion would have given much to see the Huns' faces when they looked across and found that long line of serpentine earth and wire shoved out under their noses. There would probably be some court-martialling of their patrols. Everything worked in absolute harmony, and with perfect success, and all got back safe to tell the tale. The Hun discovered what had been done only the following morning when all was over.

The lack of the more strenuous forms of active service excitement during the digging of this trench was more than made up for in the week following—when it was manned nightly in full strength, in spite of severe bombardment by the enemy.

After the successful and useful piece of work in advancing the line just described, the Battalion settled down to a period of normal trench warfare and intensive training, but managed to slip in a game of rugger and an Association game or two. Intermittent spells of artillery and trench mortar and gas shell bombardments of varying severity disturbed the sector, but despite this the unit not only immediately repaired any damage done, but considerably extended and improved the system.

On the 9th of February the shelling became very heavy, culminating towards evening in an intense bombardment on the sector lying to the left of F1. At the same time an attempt was made to neutralise the fire of the British batteries on the Ancre by gas shells. Intense excitement prevailed in the Battalion, which was billeted in Aveluy, in Brigade support, when it was called on to "stand to" and man the bridge-head defences. Meantime the Hun carried out a raid on a part of the line known as the Nab, which was occupied by the 2nd K.O.Y.L.I. This point was occupied for half-an-hour or so by the enemy, who picked up about eleven K.O.Y.L.I. prisoners and then retired. The K.O.Y.L.I. suffered some sixty casualties in killed, wounded and missing, so "B" Company and part of "C" of the 17th were rushed up into the raided sector to reinforce the battered garrison, and stayed there till morning.

Again the conditions stereotyped themselves into that nerve racking ordeal known to the civilian public as "nothing to report"—the type of warfare recognised by all who have any experience of modern active service life as calling for all that is highest in regimental efficiency and discipline, and individual initiative and grit. The weather, taking it all over, was wet and stormy, causing endless work in repairing the line and pumping the trenches clear of water. But the bright star in this bloody, muddy firmament was the commencement of leave, which opened about the 14th February. Even if your name was well down the list, or not yet even on it at all, a new species of keen counter-attraction was provided to the demands of war.

The Raid

On 17th February, 1916, the 97th Brigade was relieved by the 96th Brigade, and consequently the Battalion moved back for an expected rest of some weeks. The 15th Lancashire Fusiliers took over the Battalion Sector, and the 17th went into billets at Millencourt. Many fatigues were carried out round about Albert, the principal work being the laying of cables and the improving of roads. On the 24th, quarters were changed to Henencourt and from billets into huts in the wood—most unpleasant, firstly on account of snow and frost, and then, following a thaw, on account of knee-deep mud. But a further change on the 29th to Dernancourt brought back billets good and comfortable.

The attack on Verdun had upset the plans which had been made to give the Brigade the rest which it had been anticipating, and this last move to Dernancourt brought them into the line once more, just south of Albert.

The 32nd Division, by now, with good cause, had been named by the Germans as the "Red" Division because the Hun was given no rest by the divisional artillery and constant raids, and on account of the red distinguishing marks worn by all ranks of the Division on their tunic sleeves. The 32nd took over from the 18th Division, and on the 1st of March, 1916, the Brigade was in Divisional Reserve. On the 3rd of March, the 97th Brigade relieved the 14th Brigade, the 11th Border Regiment and 2nd K.O.Y.L.I. taking over. On March 10th the 17th H.L.I. relieved the 11th Border Regiment, and so once more they were in immediate face of the enemy. This sector was in front of Becourt Château, between Fricourt and La Boiselle.

A considerable amount of wiring was done, but life here was comparatively pleasant and the return of spring much appreciated. But, unfortunately, on the 21st of March, Col. Morton was wounded at

Albert, Major Paul taking over command of the Battalion.

Working parties were heavy, and on one occasion the Bosche blew a *camouflet* while work was in progress. During this period great preparations were made for a raid, and there was keen competition for a place in the selected party. The night selected for the raid, 2nd April, however, was unfortunately bright, and this combined with the fact that the enemy, by means of listening apparatus, seemed fully aware of what was on, led to a postponement when actually in "no man's land." The hazardous work of laying the guide tape preparatory to the abandoned raid was carried out by 2nd Lieut. H. MacRobert and Corpl. J. Chapman.

This Sector was left on the 4th of April, and the Battalion, being relieved by the 2nd Scottish Rifles, of the 23rd Brigade, 8th Division, moved to Bouzincourt and went into huts vacated by the 2nd Inniskillens.

After a week's rest at Bouzincourt the Battalion returned to the line at Authuille, on 12th April, 1916, the 97th Brigade holding the line between that village and north to Thiepval, with the two other Brigades behind, in support and in reserve. Alternately in the line, in support, and in reserve, the 17th remained in this Sector until the opening of the Somme Battle on 1st July, 1916. But the period was not without stirring incident. By the 15th of April final arrangements were being made to carry out what was to prove a highly successful raid on the enemy, which operation was accomplished on 22nd April.

23rd April, 1916,—Last night we made a successful raid against the enemy's trenches, south-west of Thiepval. Thirteen prisoners were captured, and in addition, a number of casualties were caused to the enemy by our men bombing their dug-outs. Our casualties were very slight.

This bald official statement of the 17th H.L.I.'s first raid is to the lay mind singularly unimpressive, but behind it there is an interest and a measure of glory of which the 17th is happy to be proud. Let it be remembered that it was their first "stunt," their first real hand to hand brush with the enemy, and that to the 17th fell the honour of getting the first "jab in" for the 32nd Division.

It was on the 28th of March, 1916, that volunteers were called for to raid the enemy's trenches, and out of the hundred who answered, a party of 45 was selected, under Lieut. A.J. Begg, and Lieut.

45

THE CATHEDRAL, ALBERT—BEFORE THE WAR.

THE CATHEDRAL, ALBERT—AFTER BOMBARDMENT.

Lt.-Col. David S. Morton, V.D., C.M.G.

J.N. Carpenter. This party went down to Dernancourt, behind Albert, to complete the training for the raid, and the intention was to rush the enemy on the night of 2nd April. That night, however, as already explained, proved unfavourable on account of a bright moon, and the party, after crawling stealthily towards the enemy's wire were observed near his trenches and were forced to withdraw. Training was resumed at Bouzincourt, and it was decided then to have the assistance of a preliminary artillery bombardment.

A point in the enemy's salient south-west of Thiepval was selected, the wire there was cut in advance by the artillery, and close observation was maintained on the spot from day to day. Meanwhile the enemy's fortifications were duplicated on the ground behind Bouzincourt, and there, night after night, the raiding party practised the assault. The most careful preparations were entailed, with much planning and understanding of detail. Every man had to know thoroughly his part. There had to be no hitch anywhere. Lieut. Begg saw to it that the training was complete, and given any luck, success was fully assured.

On the night of the 22nd of April, the party, with blackened hands and faces, and equipped with an assortment of weapons worthy of Mexican outlaws, presented themselves at the head of Thiepval Avenue, and filed up to the "starting point" to await the report of the Patrol under Lieut. MacRobert, who also had charge of the tape-laying party which included Corporal Chapman. At 9.30 p.m. our artillery suddenly opened on the enemy's salient, and poured down on it such a tornado of steel as the Germans had never experienced before. For twenty minutes our shells flayed the German front line, and under this arch of shrieking explosives the battle party crawled right up to the rim of the bombardment. What wire remained uncut was blown to fragments by a torpedo, and when the barrage lifted and came down behind, the raiders jumped into the enemy's trench and set to work.

For twenty minutes they bombed and destroyed, cleared dugouts, pulled down machine guns, barricaded communication trenches, and handed prisoners back to escorts. Then on a signal they as quickly withdrew, and still under cover of artillery fire made their own trench again. Thirteen affrighted Germans, of two different units, accompanied the party; and, finest of all, every man of the party returned. Eleven of them were wounded, but only one seriously. Among those slightly wounded was Lieut. Begg, who was the spirit of the assault.

As a result of this success many congratulatory messages were received and several decorations awarded. Among the list of telegrams were the following:—

From the G.O.C. 10th Corps:—

> Corps Commander congratulates the 17th H.L.I. on their successful enterprise, which reflects great credit on all concerned.

From the G.O.C. 32nd Division:—

> I congratulate you. I was confident that the 17th H.L.I. would do the trick. Convey this message to them.

From Sir Henry Rawlinson, G.O.C. 4th Army:—

> Please convey to 32nd Division, and particularly to the 97th Brigade and 17th Battalion Highland Light Infantry, my heartiest congratulations on their successful raid last night. The preparations were well and carefully thought out, the Artillery support was good, and the whole conduct of the operations reflects credit on all concerned.

From the G.O.C. 97th Infantry Brigade:—

> Commander-in-Chief has awarded the following decorations:— Lieut. Begg, and 2nd Lieut Carpenter, Military Cross; 15507 Sergt.-Major Reith, D.C.M.; 15458 Sergeant Taylor, 2797 Private Leiper and 15720 Private M'Intosh, Military Medal. All 17th H.L.I. Major-General Rycroft offers his heartiest congratulations to above officers, N.C.O.s and men on their decorations. Letter with authority following.

The Battalion had three men killed and four wounded during enemy retaliation, but any serious effort by the enemy was checked, and on the 24th the unit went into reserve billets at Bouzincourt.

A Lull Before the Storm

On 27th April, in brilliant summer weather, the Commanding Officer, Company Commanders, the Intelligence Officer and four N.C.O.s per Company attended a Divisional Exercise at Baizieux, and this was the start of those preparations which were to culminate in the Battle of the Somme on 1st July.

On 3rd May the Colonel returned and took over command from Major Paul, and during the following day, Major Lawder, Commanding "A" Battery, 168th Brigade, R.F.A., entertained those who had taken part in the raid and allowed them to fire the guns which had rendered such fine support during the sortie.

Identification marks had now been issued for some time for major operations pending. The Divisional colours were crimson and the sleeve mark was a red circle for the 97th Brigade. The K.O.Y.L.I. had one bar below the circle; the Border Regiment, two; the 16th H.L.I., three; and the 17th, four bars, worn horizontally and parallel. Runners, bombers, etc., had further identification marks. Prior to this, from November 1915, to April, 1916, no distinctive mark had been worn on the sleeve, but on the centre of the tunic collar at the back there was worn a strip of ribbon coloured yellow, pale blue, and yellow. During the succeeding period, up to the disbandment of the Battalion, the sleeve marks were used only. While the circle was always red the bars were coloured respectively black for Headquarters; red for "A" Company; green for "B"; yellow for "C"; and blue for "D" Company. The Divisional sign on flags and limbers, etc., was a red coloured intertwined double 8.

The weather was now very fine, and when not in the line, delightful days were spent at Rubempré, Contay and Warloy, and strenuous days on Divisional exercises at Baizieux in preparation for the Somme. From this it will be seen that the Battalion was not engaged in killing

Germans all the time, or being killed by them. At times they had a change. There were periods of rest. The word "rest" is very often the subject of sarcastic humour amongst troops. "Resting" may mean anything. It may be quite a good time or it may be worse than the firing line. Too often it is simply an occasion of smartening up—guards, ceremonial parades, saluting, and "spit and polish" generally—in fact the things that can be indulged in to excess. And very often a rest simply means preparation for a big stunt.

But the 17th will remember occasions when they did have a real rest. This was particularly the case at Rubempré. The weather was good, and they had a comparatively easy time. They had about three hours' training in the forenoons. Thereafter they were free. There were sports and games in the afternoons for the enthusiasts. There were entirely successful concerts and sing-songs in the evenings. It was a change to see and be among civilians—to be welcome in the village houses—and generally to experience peace time conditions again. This may not seem to amount to very much, but it meant a lot then. And it certainly had a fine effect on the morale of the Battalion. It was a sheer relief to be out of sound of the guns, to forget the mud, the exhaustion, mental and physical, the weary night watches, standing to, and working parties.

But such days passed quickly, and all too soon they found themselves on the road again, loaded up, silent, thoughtful, on the way back to the firing line.

The Battle of the Somme

Signs of the coming conflict were everywhere. The tremendous accumulation of men and material had been going on unceasingly for weeks, and during the long June days clouds of dust hung in the hot, still air above the roads. For the roads all led towards the line, and the tramp of men, and the rumble of wheels were unending. The Battalion had long ago recovered from a hard and monotonous winter of trench warfare. To each man there remained the joy of remembering days and nights that were unpleasant—for it is a joy to remember, in the comfort and happiness of today, the discomforts and sorrows of yesterday. Now the sun was shining. Training was going on apace under the pleasantest of conditions. They were a healthy family. Each man felt his potentiality, and unconsciously boasted it in his every action. Such was the feeling in the Battalion when the certainty of conflict came.

To everyone it was the "Big Push"—the mighty Armageddon—of which all had thought and spoken during the winter of waiting. There was no doubt as to the issue. Each man went about his duties with an eye to an immediate and definite future. If anything he gave greater care to his rifle. In his feeling the edge and point of his bayonet, there was something of a caress. Now was the look in each eye born of the lust of killing. It was the knowledge that on a bright morning—now only a few hours distant—man would be matched against man. "Justice of our cause may have been somewhere in our sub-consciousness. Certainly it was not uppermost. To each man the coming conflict savoured of individual mortal combat. The days of waiting were gone. He was going forward to prove his manhood"—so write two veterans of that fight.

The story of that morning is an epic. For every man it was the first experience of "over the top." In sun-baked trenches everyone longed for the zero hour, while the guns rolled and shells crashed with ever-increasing intensity. Nothing was real. Men stood and waited as if in a dream. They felt as if they were listening to the overture; that soon the curtain would rise. Even when the guns ceased their roar for a few moments towards the end, and in the death-like stillness was heard the warbling of birds in "no man's land"—the grim reality of it all was felt. With the lifting mist of the morning, the curtain rose. . . .

At 7.23 a.m. the Battalion started moving across "no man's land." When the barrage lifted the men entered the enemy front line and the work of the moppers-up soon began. The advance across the open was splendidly carried out, all ranks behaving magnificently, as was the case throughout the entire action. Leipzig Trench was taken and the leading lines advanced against the Hindenburg Trench. These were mown down and by 8.15 a.m. every Company Officer was a casualty. It now became obvious to Colonel Morton that Leipzig Trench must be held, as without reinforcements, no further advance could be made, both flanks being exposed, as the 8th Division on their right had been driven back.

The left was particularly exposed and parties under Sergt. Macgregor and Sergt. Watt were organised and sent to strengthen the left where "B" and "D" Companies had been almost annihilated. It was now 9 o'clock and the Battalion casualties now amounted to 22 officers and 400 other ranks. The bombers, who had been sent up to replace casualties, were holding the flanks successfully. By 11.15 the entire line was very weak, and still at 2 o'clock in the afternoon the situation was unchanged, 2nd Lieut. Morrison and 2nd Lieut. Marr working and organising the protective flank bombers without the least regard for personal safety. At 4 o'clock the 2nd Manchesters reinforced them with two Companies. Just at this time the line wavered a little in face of the overwhelming bombardment and the appalling casualties, but control was immediately gained.

At 5 the shattered unit was ordered to consolidate the ground taken. This was done and two strong enemy counter attacks repulsed. At 9.30 the Battalion started to be relieved by the Manchesters, but the relief was not wholly carried out until near midnight, although several bombing parties had to carry on till well towards mid-day of the following day before being relieved. The 17th concentrated on Campbell Post and held the line in that Sector. In the evening of the next day the Battalion was relieved and returned to dugouts at Crucifix Corner.

The first V.C., not only for the Battalion, but of the division was

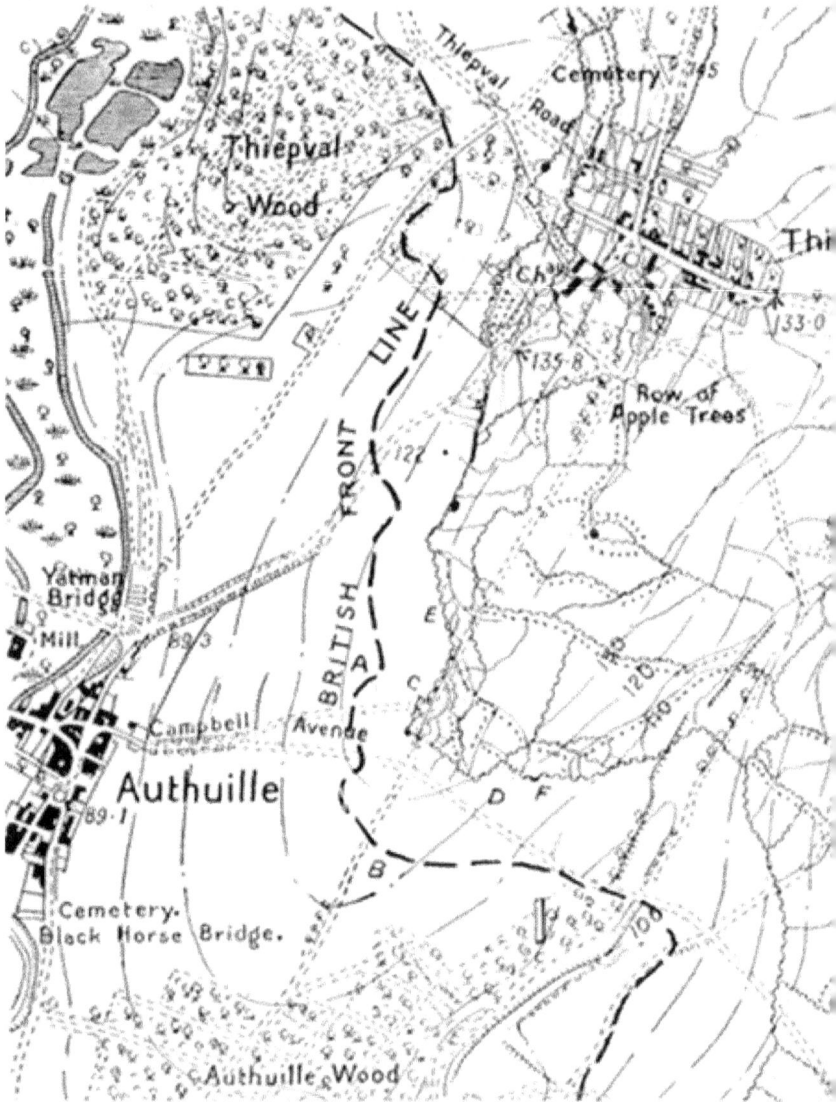

Objective of Attack—Mouquet Farm.
First German Line attacked and taken, C—D.
Trench Line from which the attack was launched, A—B.
Second German Line taken and lost, E—F.

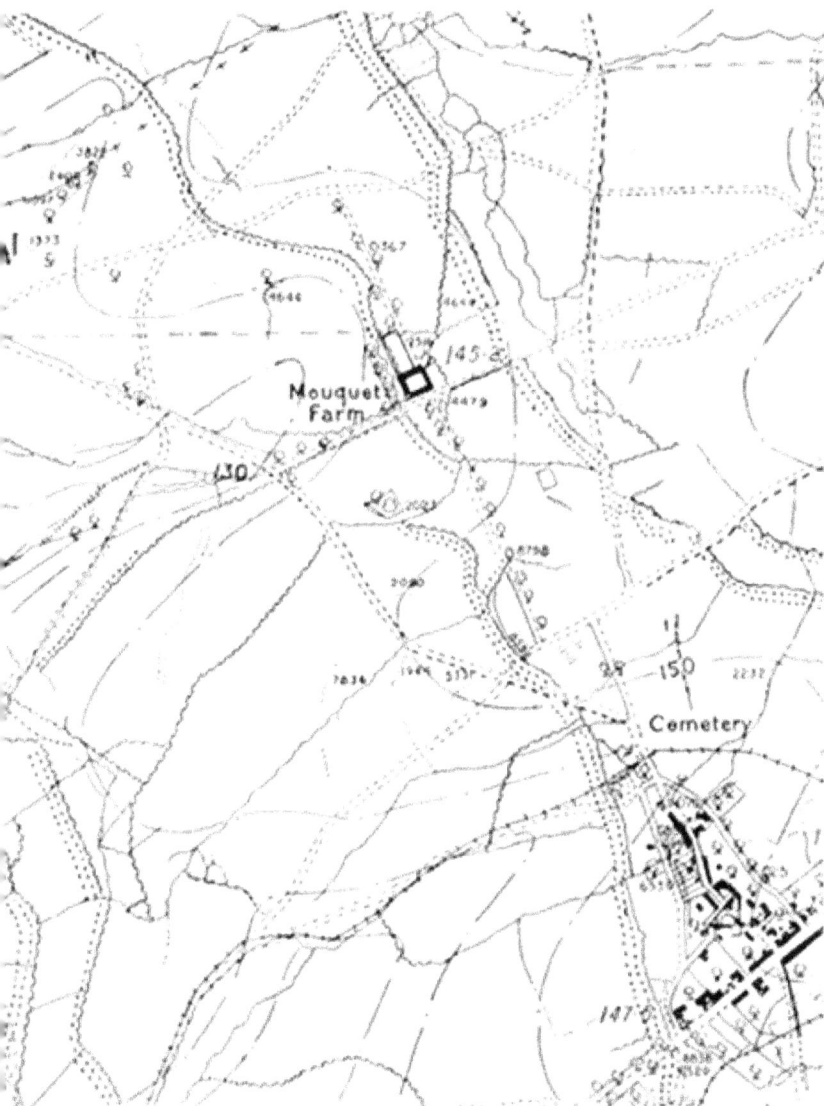

Note the Salient C—D and its exposure to German fire
and attack on the Flanks.

gained in this battle and was won by Sergeant James Young Turnbull.

The following is the extract from *The London Gazette*, of 25th December, 1916, intimating the award of the Victoria Cross:—

No. 15888 Sergeant James Young Turnbull,
late Highland Light Infantry.

For most conspicuous bravery and devotion to duty, when, having with his party captured a post apparently of great importance to the enemy, he was subjected to severe counter attacks, which were continuous throughout the whole day. Although his party was wiped out and replaced several times during the day, Sergeant Turnbull never wavered in his determination to hold the post, the loss of which would have been very serious. Almost single-handed he maintained his position and displayed the highest degree of valour and skill in the performance of his duties.

Later in the day this gallant soldier was killed whilst bombing a counter-attack from the *parados* of our trench.

Of all the units operating in that ghastly Sector, the 17th H.L.I. was the only Battalion which reached and occupied and held the enemy's trenches from La Boiselle northwards. Sir Arthur Conan Doyle, writing of the battle of the Somme in his history of the war, emphasises what this unadorned record of the day's fighting bears out—that there had been no flinching anywhere, and the military virtue shown had been of the highest possible quality; but the losses from the machine guns and from the barrage was so heavy that they deprived the attack of the weight and momentum necessary to win their way through the enemy's position. "In the desperate circumstances," he says, "it might well be considered a remarkable result that a stretch of the Leipzig Redoubt should be won and permanently held by the Highlanders, especially by the 17th Highland Light Infantry."

Throughout these terrible operations Colonel Morton was present in the most advanced positions encouraging and cheering the men by his personal example and utter disregard for danger. In this work he was gallantly seconded by his adjutant and his Headquarters' Staff, who were individually forward directing operations when all the company officers had been knocked out. it is not too much to say that the resolute spirit and example of the colonel rallied the Battalion to heights of endurance and endeavour which found their greatest inspiration in his presence in the firing line.

Great work was also done by Captain D.C. Evans, R.A.M.C., who, for over forty-eight hours, without interval or rest, attended to the Battalion wounded. Throughout the action he carried on his task of relieving suffering and saving life quite heedless of the shelling and firing and quite cool in the face of the ever growing number of cases demanding his attention and skill.

At the Battalion parade for Roll Call on the 4th of July, the casualties totalled 22 officers and 447 other ranks.

A Diary Account of the Battle

The narrative of the 1st of July Somme Battle as written in the diary of the late 2nd Lieut. B. Meadows, who, before taking his commission, served with the 17th H.L.I., gives such an impressive account of the battle that we include it here almost in entirety. The foregoing chapter gives a general idea of the intensity of the great battle from the impersonal and official viewpoint, with data checked and balanced. But the following account introduces the personal and human element with poignant effect. Some of the very minor facts are a little inaccurate, but that is inevitable when an individual soldier describes a general action from his own viewpoint. Nevertheless the editors consider that in no other Battalion source is there such a vivid record of experiences to be got which reflect the feelings of all those who took part in the action concerned.

"The last four days before zero," he writes, "were known as 'W,' 'X,' 'Y,' and 'Z' days. By 'W' every enemy observation balloon had been destroyed and so dense a fleet of aircraft patrolled the battle area as to make it impossible for the enemy aircraft to approach the lines. Thus the enemy was made blind. On the night of 'W' we got orders to move forward. Before leaving the billet we made a large bonfire with boxes from the C.Q.M.'s stores. On this we burned all our letters, and round it we had the last sing-song the old 'Seventeenth' ever had. We then believed it 'Y' night, not 'W' night. The night before we had gone up to the trenches through Aveluy and Authuille with petrol tins full of water. These were stocked in dugouts and along the trench and formed our reserve water supply.

"Many of our guns were firing 'gun fire,' yet the enemy made little artillery reply. He retaliated chiefly on the front line defences with trench mortars. Of such a violent nature was this bombardment that the Lonsdales had to call on our 'D' Company for support to make up for their casualties in shell shock, etc. Curiously enough, during the days 'D' Company held the line they suffered no casualties, although the trench was battered out of all recognition. When it was dark on 'W' night we marched to Bouzincourt. Here we spent the night in huts. Before daybreak we were shelled and had one man killed. Day showed an extraordinary sight. Bouzincourt stands on the hill, the battle area stretched out like a map below. Near the Crucifix on the Aveluy road a long naval gun barked. Just behind us was a 15 inch howitzer. Its shells could easily be watched in their flight overhead. In front were an infinite number of guns all in action.

"A long line of observation balloons made a crescent round Albert. One could count over twenty, and not one German. The air was thick with our aeroplanes. The German lines looked like long ribbons of white fur. The air was full of shrapnel balls, especially over the woods, and the villages were burning. The heavy howitzers were causing dreadful eruptions on the German strong points. La Boisselle, believed impregnable, was a concentrated hell. The Germans were putting shrapnel into the woods that lie in the triangle between Hamel, Bouzincourt and Aveluy. Here our guns were massed. And now and then a mushroom of smoke would spring up in unexpected places. The noise was so terrific that it became monotonous.

"We were served out with cotton wool for our ears, but in spite of this the concussion on the 1st of July was so great that we all became stone deaf, and for days after almost without the use of our voices. We prepared for 'battle order.' All our belongings we packed into our valises, and these were stored in an empty house in Bouzincourt. We wore steel helmets, at that time they were without sandbag coverings, and in strong sunlight reflected almost as brilliantly as polished steel. I noticed on the 1st July, looking back from the advanced line to the German original front line, how the helmets of our reserves holding that line shone up and made their wearers clear targets. We wore the haversack on our back containing mess tin, small kit, two days' rations, 'iron rations,' pair of socks and waterproof sheet.

"We carried four sandbags just below. Then we had the usual equipment, pouches containing 120 rounds, bayonet, water bottle and entrenching tool. Another 100 rounds in bandoliers, and I had extra an apron containing 12 Mill's bombs and butterfly wirecutters. The whole formed fairly heavy equipment. In the late afternoon when we were all lined up prepared to march off, orders came to cancel all orders. We stood by for two days. On 'X' night the 16th H.L.I. sent a platoon over to find out the condition of the enemy defences.

"Owing to an accident they were almost entirely wiped out. On the following morning while playing a football match the Sixteenth again suffered casualties from a 5.9 which burst between the goal posts. In the evening of 'Z' day, the 30th of June, we marched off by platoons. The thunder of the heavy guns as we passed through their belt was almost unbearable, and nearer the lines long lines of eighteen-pounders were giving 'battery fire' down long rows of twenty batteries, sometimes all speaking at once. We entered 'Oban Avenue' at the right end of the village of Authuille. It was the 'up' trench for the advance and 'Campbell Avenue' the 'down.' Both trenches had been deepened, in some places, to twelve feet, and were fairly safe from shrapnel. The line in which we were to spend the night had been blown almost completely out of existence and it was difficult to find sufficient cover for the men.

"I and the bomber who was next to me in the line found a corner and there slept for the night. We were once disturbed by the enemy destroying a trench mortar store situated close to where we slept. Daybreak came and still there was no word of 'zero.' We made some breakfast, and about half-past five word was passed along that zero was 7.30, and to move into battle positions. We moved to the right until we were in contact with the next Company. At 6.25 a.m. the final bombardment commenced. Every gun was firing 'gunfire' and the rush of metal overhead was extraordinary. The reply was feeble. At 7.25 we left the trench and walked over to within 60 yards of the barrage. At 7.30 the barrage lifted and we rushed the front line defences, destroying the garrison, in and out of dugouts.

"I have few definite memories from the time we first saw the Germans to the time the machine gun swept us down outside the Liepzig Redoubt. It became evident that we, who were working up between two communication trenches, after two or three rushes, that further advancing was impossible without support. We waited for our own reserve waves and the Lonsdales who should have come on behind. But no reserves reached us and we saw our only hope lay in the fact that they had rushed one of the communication trenches and might manage to bomb out the machine gun. But the bombers were checked out of range of the gun.

"We began to work towards the communication trench, but owing to the lie of the ground we were badly exposed and I at length found myself the only living occupant of that corner. About twelve o'clock

I managed to leap the parapet without being hit. I found my platoon officer, Lieut. MacBrayne, lying shot through the head. Of the others of my platoon I could get no news, except those I saw lying dead or wounded. Tom Train had completely disappeared. An order came up the trench, '17th H.L.I. move to the left and prepare to support the Dorsets.' The communication trench was at this time chiefly manned by K.O.Y.L.I. (who should have supported the 16th H.L.I. who had been held up by the German wire and cut up before able to take the first line of defences.

"Those left were forced to retire to their own line). A few Lonsdales (the 11th Borderers had been cut up coming up through 'Blighty Wood,' colonel and adjutant killed and all officers casualties) were able to give us practically no support, and a company of Manchesters, sent from Divisional Reserve. I moved to the left. An officer suddenly jumped the parapet and shouted 'Come on, the 17th!' I followed him along with about twenty others. But we found the barbed wire impossible to cut through and he gave us the order 'Every man for himself.'

"Making my way back to the trench I rested in a shell hole occupied by a Sergeant wounded in the leg. Whilst talking to him we both fell asleep and slept until about 5 p.m., when the Germans counterattacked. Their artillery became violent and they attempted to come over the open. We ran for the communication trench and found it disorganised. Orders got mixed and some seemed anxious to retire. Fortunately the 17th H.L.I. bombers, who were in the advanced position, held their ground, driving the enemy back with their own bombs, and the attack over the open was checked by our brigade machine guns which had been massed in the German front line. During the whole action we lost no ground that had previously been gained. By this time our Battalion had been badly hit. 'B' Company on our left had been caught in the wire and cut to pieces by machine gun fire. My own Company, 'A,' was down to low numbers.

"My captain and my platoon officer were both killed, all the platoon's N.C.O.s were killed or wounded, two sergeants outright, and all the l.-corpls. dead. We had 17 officers killed and were working the Battalion with two officers. The colonel, who had been well forward all day, was without a scratch. It was a remarkably clear day, very hot. We were on the ridge that formed the defence on that side of Thiepval. From here we could see the whole battlefield. I saw the huge eruption at La Boisselle, when the six mines went up, and I remember watching long lines of Highlanders charging along the opposite slope

PART OF THIEPVAL. 17TH H.L.I. BAPAUME. BECOURT WOOD. BRITISH OBSERVATION BALLOONS.
LINE ATTACKED. (Front Line OVILLERS.
Trench). LA BOISSELLE.

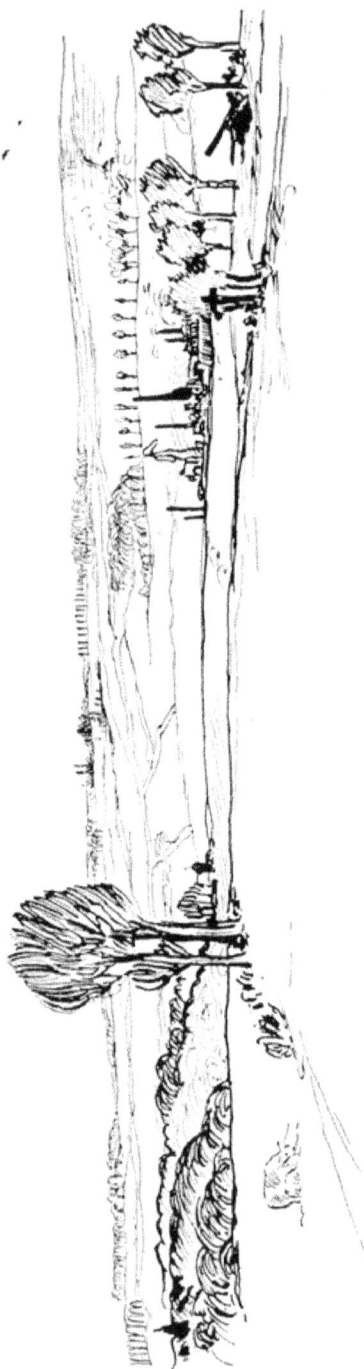

AVELUY WOOD. BLIGHTY WOOD. ALBERT.
CRUCIFIX CORNER. AVELUY ROAD.

VIEW FROM BOUZINCOURT LOOKING TOWARDS THE LINE.
(*Sketch from Lieut. Meadow's Diary*).

of the valley.

"The aeroplanes followed every movement, flying low overhead and directing the artillery by dropping flares. The Germans counter-attacked in a half-hearted way through the night. We had casualties from our own artillery and mortar batteries, otherwise the night was quieter than we had expected. We managed to carry away a number of our wounded in waterproof sheets. The battalions on both flanks were unsuccessful in storming the enemy's front line defences, thus our flanks were exposed and blockades had to be formed at the front line and all lines forward to our advanced positions, which developed into a series of bombing posts. Local fights went on at their posts all through the day and night, and it was while chasing each other round corners at the head of the communication trench in the afternoon that we lost Sergeant Turnbull, V.C., who had done wonderful work all day.

"The nature of the Leipzig defences, a maze of trenches and under-ground saps, made advancing into the salient extremely hard. One was continually attacked in the rear. What seemed dugouts were bombed, and when passed numbers of the enemy rush from them, they being really underground communications with their rear defences. The whole fighting was of a cold, deliberate, merciless nature. No quarter was given or taken. One of the battalions opposing us was similar to our own, a students' battalion from Bavaria. The enemy used explosive and dum-dum bullets, and sniped off any of our wounded lying exposed in the open. They were helped in their work by an arrangement we had come to regarding wounded. It was not permitted to stop to take back prisoners or to stop to dress a wounded chum; but it was permitted to stick the bayonet of the wounded man's rifle in the ground and thus to mark the spot where he lay.

"The Germans observed this and watched for any movement in the heap beside the standing rifle. Men coolly fired at each other at point blank range, and sniping became the chief cause of casualties. It resembled a duel between two men who had had a deadly quarrel—so intensely deliberate. On the morning of the 2nd of July we handed over the front line of attack to Divisional Reserves and went into sup-port. At sunset we were relieved by the Cheshires, and moved back to the dugouts at Crucifix Corner. We had a number of casualties coming out of action. We were given tea, food and rum, and went off into a heavy sleep."

Hulluch and Thereabouts

In the sadness and stress of the first days after the Somme, there came messages round to say the Battalion was saying "Goodbye" to its colonel. Worn out with fatigue he had been reluctantly persuaded by the Brigadier and the doctors that if he wished to live and serve his country more in the war he must retire from the dreadful strain of command. In a field at Senlis, on the afternoon of 8th July, the remnants of the Battalion, on their last parade under Colonel Morton, were drawn up, silent and deeply moved. In a few words the colonel told the Battalion what he was going to do and all stood there with their losses and their heartbreaks, hardly able to keep down the tears. Addressing the men he congratulated them in warm and feeling terms for their devotion while under his command and wished them well in the uncertainties of the future.

Colonel Morton had started them, trained them, and cared for them; fought brigade and authorities for them; led them and loved them—and now they were to lose him. He said little, for much of a speech would not come, but he knew their memories and he knew what they felt. Major Paul, on behalf of the Battalion, expressed the profound regret of all ranks in losing the guidance and leadership of Colonel Morton, who had raised the 17th to such a high state of proficiency, and to wish him a well merited rest and all happiness. Just these few words of "Goodbye," then they cheered him and, with a lump in their throats they were not ashamed of, they dismissed. All said goodbye in their hearts and wished him God-speed. It is sad to part with a loved C.O. who, too, feels the parting.

Major Paul then took over command of the 17th and that evening once more they moved into the trenches in support at Quarry Post, Authuille Wood.

On the 13th July a bombing party of about 100 men were ordered to attack the German Line, north of Ovillers, linking up with the Inniskillen Fusiliers, and this party at midnight under Captain Ferguson, Lieuts. Herron and Kirk and Sergeant Stewart, in conjunction with the Inniskillens and a party of Engineers, carried out the raid.

The greatest credit was due to the initiative shown by Captain Ferguson, in making excellent dispositions under very difficult conditions. Owing to the strength of the German wire, a frontal attack was impracticable, and after much thought, it was decided to attack obliquely. The attack was most successful, a considerable number of Germans being killed, while at least 16 were taken prisoners. The objectives were all taken in a few minutes, but unfortunately the raiders' losses were heavy. Captain Ferguson was mortally wounded, eight other ranks were killed, and the other two officers and about 35 other ranks were wounded.

Writing of this incident, one of the Battalion officers says that after the patrol had gone out those who were not taking part in it heard the firing and the clamour of the small battle while they waited eagerly for news of its progress. "News came in that the front was safe, and proud of the efforts of our Battalion, we waited for their return. The waiting was hard to bear, but the return sadder to witness. They came back. On the right they had succeeded. On the left they had died. A triumph and a disaster in one. On that small field were left yet more of the (oh! so sadly few) gallant men of the Seventeenth who, though exhausted and battle-worn, had in their own true and fine spirit responded to the uttermost to the call for gallant work. Later the body of Captain Ferguson was found right up to the German lines grasping an empty revolver, far ahead in the charge of even his gallant followers."

For this action, the Battalion received thanks and congratulations from the corps and division. A counter-attack drove the raiders out of the captured trench; but the object of the raid—to create a diversion from a major operation on the right—had been successfully accomplished.

This particular week, which was the last the Battalion saw of the Somme fighting until later in the year, was one of the most strenuous times which the unit had experienced. The available men for defensive purposes were only too few and as new assembly trenches had to be dug every night and all night, and also owing to the difficulties of rationing and watering, the men were unable to get any rest.

The brigade commenced a move to Ampliers on 16th July, and on the road the Battalion was met by Lieut.-General T.L.N. Moreland, commanding the X Corps. He expressed to the commanding officer his appreciation of the good work done by the Battalion while under his command, and his deepest sympathy in their losses. On the 26th the Brigade moved into Bethune and two days afterwards paraded in full marching order, including "tin hats," on a sweltering afternoon, to be inspected by General Munro, G.O.C., 1st Army. A very warm day. Owing to the calls on an Army Commander's time, this inspection was considered to be a great honour and a mark of appreciation by the authorities of the fine spirit shown by the Division during the Somme battle.

August saw the unit leave Bethune to take over the Cambrin right sub-sector from the Northamptons, after putting in some fine shooting on the old French Government Rifle Range at Labeauvriere. The strength of the unit in the trenches apart from the officers, at the taking over (August 5th) was 199—tragic testimony to the Somme. Immediately on taking over the trenches they were subjected to trench mortar bombardments and sniping raids. On 12th August Lieut. and Adjutant Paterson became captain and adjutant, Major Paul became lieut.-colonel, and 2nd Lieuts. Morrison and Marr, captains.

The following weeks of August, September and October were marked with much moving about with various spells of that sort of uneventful trench warfare which is perhaps in some respects more trying on the nerves and strength of a unit than actual operations. On August 23rd they were in the Hulluch Section. In this section there was a good deal of mining going on and there were two big craters which required special watching, but the Battalion soon set to and trained in grappling hook work to be ready for any kind of crater fighting that might be demanded of them.

On August 31st a move was made to Annequin *via* Beuvry and Bethune, and ultimately by bus journey to the trenches at Guinchy left sub-section, and in this area the unit remained during September. On the 11th of the month a night raid was attempted, but was frustrated owing to the Germans bombing the party as it was on the point of entering their trenches. Unfortunately the two N.C.O.s who fired the torpedo were missing, and it is presumed that they were blown to bits by the explosion.

On October 4th the Battalion took over "Village Trench" in the Cambrin Sector (Maison Rouge), taking over the front line from the 11th Border Regiment. The next move saw the 17th leave Beuvry

COOKHOUSE AT BECOURT.

OBSERVATION POST, HULLUCH SECTOR.

WAR'S DESTRUCTION.

LIEUT.-COLONEL W.J. PAUL.

and proceeding to Labeauvriere on October 16th; to Hardinval, on the 19th; to Rubempré, on the 21st; to Bouzincourt, on the 23rd; back by Rubempré and on to Canaples on the 31st *via* Talmas and Navurs. This treking was done in weather that was oftener wet than dry, exceedingly cold at night, and the living was under canvas. At Val-de-Maison on November 1st, the unit moved to Vadencourt after a fortnight, and then into the Martinsart Valley on the 15th, where they were ordered to go into action at Beaumont-Hamel, for by this time several drafts had brought up the strength of the Battalion.

Beaumont-Hamel

The attack which commenced at ten minutes past six on the morning on November 18th—a day of ice-covered slushiness—was held up owing to the insufficiency of the artillery barrage and the heavy enemy machine gun fire. At 7.42 a.m. the message came in to the Battalion from the right hand company that the company commander was wounded and that a sergeant and about ten men were holding the right flank. The jumping off trench known as New Munich Trench, was manned by the Battalion machine gunners with a view to concentrating some of the companies in it back across "no man's land" to form a rallying point. At 8.30 a.m. the following message was received from 2nd Lieut. Macbeth of the right company:

> Am holding old front line with remainder of Battalion, and have established a bombing post on the right. There are only Lieut. Martin and myself in the trench.

The left company was also being hard pressed. It was reported by one of the Battalion officers that when the barrage opened a great number of shells fell just in front of New Munich Trench where the attacking companies were lying out, killing and wounding a large number of the Battalion. When the barrage lifted on to Munich Trench for the last four minutes, it was still short, and when the leading waves came up to about 50 or 60 yards from Munich Trench followed by the barrage, the Germans could be seen lying in the trench in force. When the barrage was on the Munich Trench, the enemy machine guns played on the attackers from both flanks all the time. The failure of the attack was due to the inefficiency of the British supporting barrage, together with the condition of the ground—thaw having set in and rain falling on the snow, making it exceedingly slippery—the targets the men formed against the snowy background, and the intense cold.

Describing the attack one of the members of the Battalion

writes:—

> The preliminary bombardment opened with its awful messages of destruction, and the rapid reply of the enemy's artillery indicated ominously that our intentions were not unknown to him. When our barrage lifted, and the first wave of our men attempted to go forward, their dark forms showed up against the snow. They were met by machine gun fire, by rapid fire from the enemy trenches, and by snipers in skilfully chosen holes. Our bombardment had failed. It was impossible to get to close quarters with the enemy—hopeless to advance—dangerous to retire. Many of our men were killed in the attack, others in the attempt to carry in the wounded. Many remained all day in exposed positions, beside their wounded comrades, in hope of rescuing them when darkness fell. Beaumont Hamel will not be remembered by us as bearing any resemblance to the official description. We look back upon it now, from the personal point of view, as a touchstone of the individual soul, as a prominent landmark in the vast monotony of death and horror—a chapter of inspiring deeds. It represents to us the heroism of a forlorn hope, the glory of unselfish sacrifice, the success of failure. 'Tis too easy to despond 'while the tired waves' visibly gain no 'painful inch,' hard to believe that 'far back through creeks and inlets making, comes silent, flooding in, the main.'

On the 19th the Battalion was relieved and returned to Mailly-Maillet where billets were taken over, and when the 17th rested and licked its wounds—well over 300 of "Glasgow's Own" had either been killed or wounded in that day's fighting. On the 21st of November General Gough, G.O.C. Fifth Army, inspected and congratulated the Battalion, and spoke to many of the N.C.O.s and men individually. During December the unit carried on training at Franqueville and Rubempré, and that the spirit of the men was not broken by the severity of their recent experiences is shown by the number of football matches played during the period.

On Christmas Day, 1916, the officers beat the sergeants at rugby by 11 points to 0; in the afternoon "B" Company beat Headquarters at Association by 4 goals to 0; and in the evening the Battalion held a cheery concert. The Christmas dinners were reserved for the 30th, and on Hogmanay the New Year was welcomed with a concert. General Gough attended Battalion church parade on the first Sunday of the New Year.

The New Year, 1917

The opening months of the New Year were months of battling not only against a human enemy, but against the elements and the bad conditions which they created. The winter of 1916 had been a severe one, and in passing into 1917 it continued its course with unabated severity. The Battalion left Rubempré on January 6th and partly by motor lorry and partly in column of route proceeded to Courcelles where, on the following day, they relieved the troops of the 3rd Division in the trenches opposite Serre. The weather was bad, the enemy kept up brisk attentions and the trenches were the worst which the Battalion had ever been in. Most of them were absolutely impassable, being full of water to a height of five feet, with the result that reliefs had for the most part to be made outside the trenches. Owing to this condition of matters, strict orders were issued for the prevention of "trench feet," but notwithstanding every precaution, several cases occurred.

Heavy and continuous work was put in mending and bettering the trenches, training the drafts which were arriving, performing tactical exercises and battalion routine affairs. By this time several ceremonies had taken place at which decorations were bestowed upon N.C.O.s and men for bravery in the Field and gallantry in action. *Esprit de corps* was stronger than ever, and the tediousness of trench labours was relieved by the establishment of special strong posts, by minor raids on the Bosche, and when out of the line by football and such recreations as the circumstances permitted. This type of campaigning was experienced during January and February at Courcelles, Beaumont Hamel, Lyntham Camp, Mailly-Maillet, Bolton Camp, Molliens-au-Bois (where on February 19th, 1917, Major F.R.F. Sworder, Gordon Highlanders, assumed temporary command—Colonel Paul, after being in hospital in France, having been sent to England where he was appointed to a home unit), Camon, Wiencourt, Le Quesnel. And in March, the approach of spring seemed to bring with it nothing but additional storms of rain and snow, and the names of such points in the line as Key Post and Kuropatkin will bring back memories of buttressing up collapsed trenches and mending wire entanglements.

But the opening of the 1917 Spring Offensive soon gave a great fillip to activities. The French attacked on March 16th and the 96th Brigade attacked with it. The enemy was forced back so rapidly that by 2 o'clock on the day following the Allied artillery was out of range, and the day after that again saw the whole Battalion hard at it clearing wire from the road running through the enemy's old front system, and setting out on the march, complete with transport, at 5 in the morning. Arriving at Nesle on March 19th, the troops were given a tremendous welcome by the French populace. It was discovered there that the people were literally starving, because the Germans had taken their rations for some days previously.

A dam on the Somme burst its banks and no advance was possible until this was repaired and new roads made across the floods, but it was only a few days until once more the troops were pushing on and the commanding officer and company commanders of the 17th were making a reconnaissance of the new main position at Germaine. The digging at Germaine on March 28th was one of the heaviest day's work ever done by the Battalion. The job commenced at night, after an 18 mile march in rain and finished in snow. The digging was covered by the 16th H.L.I., who held the outpost line. The newly dug trenches were shelled on the following forenoon.

On the Heels of the Enemy

The Battalion moved off from Germaine at midnight on April 1st, 1917, and proceeded by companies at 200 yard intervals cross country to Fluquieres. Arriving there they passed through the village, a pile of smouldering ruins, and on the main St. Quentin road and about half a mile along it they reached Roupy with its destroyed cross-roads and proceeded towards a point near Savy where the Battalion deployed, and attacking at 5 a.m. moved forward, overcame the opposition and took Savy. In the village the Bosche put up a desperate stand and some fierce fighting took place before they were pushed beyond the railway bank north of the village. Most of the fighting took place in the neighbourhood of an orchard at the southern end of the village, and here the 11th Border Regiment joined forces in helping to drive out the stubborn enemy.

Once through the village serious destruction was caused by heavy machine gun fire from an enemy strong point in a mine crater. With the aid of two Lewis guns, the crater was soon in the hands of the 17th and a heavy fire directed on the retreating enemy. Thereafter the Battalion started to dig in (about 6.30 a.m.), and soon consolidated their gains, although subject to strong artillery, machine gun and sniping fire. In the afternoon a further attack was made by the 96th Brigade, and before evening Bois-de-Savy was in their hands. The Battalion was relieved in the evening and moved off to take up quarters in dug-outs on the Fluquieres-Douchy Road, but the place had been so badly knocked about that a large portion of the unit bivouacked.

The total casualties in this day's fighting was 103, 31 of whom were killed. During the following week the Battalion suffered from the severe winter conditions, coupled with incessant shelling and had much to do strengthening their positions. On the 9th some magnificent patrolling was done, for which the Battalion was deservedly congratulated. In the afternoon of that day four patrols set out to gain information of Fayet and the ground between Francilly and St. Quentin. One patrol went to the ridge overlooking St. Quentin, one went into a German trench near Fayet, one went within 300 yards of Fayet, and the fourth reconnoitred the southern approaches of the village—and much valuable information was accordingly gained.

On the 12th April, Major Lumsden, V.C., D.S.O., who was in temporary command of the Battalion, relinquished that post, to take up duty as Brigadier-General of the 14th Infantry Brigade—which this very distinguished officer commanded until he was killed—and Captain Morton assumed command of the Battalion, with Captain Paterson, M.C., as second in command.

While at Holnon on the 13th, "C" and "D" Companies were sent forward in support of the 2nd K.O.Y.L.I., who were attacking Fayet. This attack was carried out in conjunction with one being made by the French, who were endeavouring to take St. Quentin. "B" Company joined the others in the front line, and later the Battalion took over a sector of the front line. After consolidating here, congratulatory messages were received from Brigadier-General Blacklock, General Shute and General Rawlinson.

The road from Nesle to St. Quentin is a long and cruel one, but in these early days of 1917, it was to the 17th H.L.I. the pathway to glory. They were sweeping onwards in the track of the retreating enemy, with the glow of victory to strengthen their hearts and the blessings of a delivered people in their ears. The echoing trumpets of romance called to them from the Cathedral City, and their blood stirred to the call. These were the impressions that led them, in common with the rest of the division, to surmount appalling obstacles, natural and devilish. They soaked in the snow, and froze in the keen blast; they starved and toiled on the way, but "stuck it," and their reward was the fall of Savy village. There was fighting all along the 50 mile front just then, and Savy did not loom very large in the chronicles of the time, but those who took part in its capture, and in the taking of the wood a mile beyond, knew that they had achieved the heroic.

There was no resting; Francilly and Holnon were the next to fall, and the men were within sight of the spires of St. Quentin. They lived for some days in earth holes, and the weather flayed them unmercifully. Then one dark morning, the 13th of April, they assembled silently and lay down in the field, whilst dawn broke with singing of birds, and the shriek and whistle of the barrage. The division was attacking

75

Fayet, the enemy's last stronghold beyond the city. Before they went over, grey and green coated figures were being brought down. There were many other grey and green figures grotesquely contorted in the brown ribbed fields, and those of them who had escaped from the inferno fought it out intermittently, in the woods beyond the village. But their sniping was braved for a few days more, and then one night they staggered weakly back through nightmare villages to Germaine for rest.

After resting at Germaine the Battalion set off on the 19th for Canizy which was reached by evening. They found this village emptied of the native populace and saw that the Germans had been carrying out their usual work of destruction in the same wanton and deliberate scale as in nearly every village in the regained area. A more cheerful memory of this devastated village is that while here the Battalion got its new bugle band. While stationed there the Battalion marched over to Ham where a football match was to be played. Their march into the town caused great interest, and they passed through a long line of French soldiers and civilians who lined the roads.

On their approach along the main street, the square seemed totally blocked with a mass of French soldiers, and a company of infantry stood at the "present" as a Guard of Honour as they marched past the town hall, while the French band rendered our National Anthem. After the Battalion team had won their match by 6 goals to 1 against the 121st Infantry Regiment and a scratch team had played a drawn game against the 408th Regiment, the French band played the men out of the village. But the French were not allowed to have all their own way of it with the music, for the Battalion Pipe Band played to them and was received with much favour.

The regiment was in highest spirits, battle scarred and with a glorious record of great achievements established. The Battalion remained at rest in the village of Canizy until May 15th—that is, they trained hard and played hard, went marches and were inspected, performed innumerable fatigues and parades and carried out generally that never ending programme of activities which always makes a soldier smile at the mention of the word "rest!" The men played some of their keenest and most memorable games of soccer here, and one of the principle pastimes engaged in by the officers was hunting, until this was forbidden by G.H.Q.

The country, being entirely uncultivated made ideal going. Major Campbell, in charge of physical training, G.H.Q., was with the 17th for some time, and put extra life into sport and training.

On the 15th the Battalion moved off to Curchy, *via* Voyennes and Nesle, and on the succeeding day to Rosieres and so on to Hangard on the 18th, where the "resting" was carried on until the end of the month, when they proceeded to Villers-Bretonneux. Of the villages in the regained area little or no description in the normal sense is possible beyond the fact that while some semblance of streets could be traced in some of them, the majority of them were simply masses of masonry debris literally peppered with shell craters. But it was noticeable in such villages as Nesle that the civilians showed a very marked physical improvement as the result of better feeding and life under British occupation. While at Hangard, Battalion Headquarters occupied Hangard Château—one of the finest *châteaux* in France. (It was demolished during the 1918 German offensive.) The brigade concentrated at Villers-Bretonneux prior to entraining for the Second Army.

But before leaving the Fourth Army, to which the 17th had given such brilliant service, the following message was transmitted to the Battalion as one of the divisional units concerned:—

Fourth Army, No. G.S.702.

32nd Division.

As the Division will shortly be leaving the Fourth Army I desire to express to all ranks my warm thanks for the excellent services they have performed whilst under my command. The gallantry and dash displayed by the Division during the advance in March and April, especially in the actions resulting in the capture of Savy, Bois de Savy, Francilly, Holnon, Selency, Fayet and Cepy Farm, reflect the highest credit on all concerned.

The skilful leadership of all ranks, coupled with the close co-operation between Artillery, Infantry and Aircraft, was a feature in these operations deserving the highest praise, and I heartily congratulate the Division on the successes they have achieved.

I much regret that the Division is now leaving the Fourth Army, but I shall hope that at some future date I may again have the good fortune to find them under my command.

(Signed)   H. Rawlinson,
                              General, Commanding Fourth Army.

H.Q., Fourth Army,
22nd May, 1917.

In Flanders

The Battalion on 1st June, 1917, left the Fourth Army and the Somme area. The 17th never again served in that area though it served again with the Fourth Army on the sea coast. Entraining at Villers-Bretonneux the unit journeyed to Amiens and by way of Abbeville, Etaples, Boulogne, Calais, St. Omer, Hazebrouck to Steenbecque.

Owing to a mistake of the Railway transport officer an incident, upsetting but not without its amusing side, occurred at Abbeville, where the train moved off without warning while the Battalion was parading in the station for tea, with only 100 all ranks on board. The train calmly continued its journey and in due course arrived at Steenbecque, the men who were left following on in the overcrowded trucks of the 2nd Manchesters. Leaving the train at Hazebrouck, the stranded party marched to Steenbecque, their appearance, owing to deficiencies of equipment and in some cases even of uniform, causing much interested amusement. At the latter station the first party were picked up, packs and equipment donned, and then, in the afternoon the Battalion accomplished a very interesting, though long and heavy march to a small hamlet in the Donlieu area, where they billeted for ten days or so.

The 32nd Division came into the 14th Corps, commanded by the Earl of Cavan, in G.H.Q. Reserve. The 14th Corps was composed of the Guards Division, 1st, 8th and 32nd Divisions.

On 5th June the commanding officer, with his officers and N.C.O.s reconnoitred the Messines Sector with a view to supporting the attack to be carried out on the Messines-Wytschaete Ridge by the Second Army. The 17th at Donlieu "stood to" ready to move off in support of this offensive, though happily the success of the attack did not necessitate the Battalion being called on. Major Inglis of the 1st H.L.I.— who had been cross-posted to the 2nd Manchesters, which Battalion

Lt.-Col. J. Inglis, C.M.G., D.S.O.

he commanded until re-posted to command the 17th H.L.I. on the 20th of July—joined the Battalion on the 8th of June.

Donlieu was left on 14th June and the Battalion went in column of route to Steenvoorde, in which area they were billeted. This was one of the most trying marches they had experienced, and a large number of men fell out. In 6 hours the unit had covered 24 kilometres which, in full marching order, was a most difficult and wearisome performance. On the 16th the Battalion embussed outside Steenvoorde, and after leaving the charabancs at Petite Synthe, they marched to billets at Mardyck. Hereabouts was pleasant country with excellent sea bathing. Petite Synthe was left on the 19th for Dunkirk where they entrained and proceeded east along the sand dunes to Coxyde and, on the following day, into the coastal camp of Kuhn. Coxyde and Kuhn were French built camps and very good, with vegetable gardens attached to them.

Until 10th July the Battalion stayed in this vicinity, and despite spells of shelling, trench mortar and aerial bombardments, considerable patrolling and wiring work, the stay on the sand dunes about Nieuport was heaven after the endless mud and horror of the winter on the Somme. The very mention of Nieuport to a man who was there in the first week of July, 1917, makes a marked impression on his countenance. Since detraining at Coxyde on 20th June, things had been comparatively quiet and the weather ideal. Working parties were supplied for the roads during the day and smaller parties were engaged on the breastworks in the front line at night.

The quietness was absolutely awful. But the presence of civilians in Oost Dunkirk and Les Bains gave an air of security and quietude to the place which was very soothing to the heart of the soldier. It is true that aerial activity was disquieting at times, but several successful attacks on the "Vultures of the Kaiser" made these items of interest, rather than causes of alarm. The Germans seemed to pay greater attention to something well on the left of the Battalion and towards the sea, than to anything that concerned them particularly. The appearance of the roads from Oost Dunkirk to Nieuport was most assuring and their great beauty and undisturbed tranquillity were all that could be desired.

A large amount of work was attempted during this period on the Brigade Front, in order to obtain sufficient cover for protection against retaliation after our artillery bombardments began, prior to an intended attack on the sea-coast by the 4th Army, in conjunction with the 5th and 2nd Armies from Ypres. The enemy, before our artillery came in, greatly increased his artillery force, and daily destroyed any work done by night. These destructive shoots were afterwards found to be part of his barrage programme for the attack on the 10th July.

Operations on the Coast

The Battalion continued to carry out its duties on the Belgian coast until relieved from that sector on October 5th, 1917. In the previous chapter some idea of the general conditions has been given. And the period which followed was of somewhat like nature with intermittent outstanding excursions and alarms and with memorable pleasant episodes to intermix with those more combative, and in this chapter the outstanding features will be recorded without following the movements of the Battalion to the various points in this sand-dune sector.

The comparatively routine behaviour of the daily aerial and artillery "strafe" broke into a brisk and heavy bombardment on the division to the left on the night of July 9th, but on the 10th about five o'clock in the morning this heavy fire switched on to the trenches from the border of the sea to Nieuport. The bombardment crashed on to all lines, firing, reserve, and rear. It got heavier and heavier and soon reached an unprecedented violence and extended to the flanking divisions as well. The British guns replied, but could not force the hostile fire to slacken, and in the evening the enemy came on in attack. They carried the trenches of the units on the left and patrols were put out and the flank strengthened. This was the severest bombardment the Battalion had ever been in. It was a hurricane onslaught. The 17th knew that sort. They had been through it. Positions were taken and held, where no trench afforded cover, and where breastworks were blown away.

The 17th were ordered to send three companies in support of the Border Regiment who were being hard pressed east of the Yser. "A," "B" and "C" Companies were despatched on this mission. These companies experienced very stiff fighting throughout the night of the 10-11th, until relieved early in the morning of the 11th by the

Northumberland Fusiliers.

On the following day the bombardment slackened a little, though during the night hurricane fire broke out, and over the period of this attack the Hun used a very large number of tear gas shells—which at that time was a new horror introduced to the sufferings of the British armies. Who will forget the Redans, Le Grand and Le Petit, the Bridges Putney and Pelican? The last named was renewed or rebuilt on the average three times every twenty-four hours. No words can describe what took place between the 10th and 13th of that awful month. The Germans, expecting an attack, made one. After these terrible three days, the Battalion, whose luck it was on this occasion to be spared the brunt of the action, after being relieved by the Borderers, struggled back through a mixed barrage of shells of all calibres, sprinkled with those of gas. There was a fog of gas and dust for miles behind the lines.

The enemy attempt had broken down; the Battalion returned to Ghyvelde of pleasant recollection, and on the 13th the Division was congratulated on its successful efforts.

On July 20th Major J. Inglis joined the Battalion and took over command at Bray Dunes Plage. On the 23rd the Brigade was inspected by the divisional general, Major-General Shute. After his inspection he gave an address congratulating the brigade on its part against the enemy attack on the 10th inst. at Nieuport, and on the same day the corps commander also inspected the brigade, complimenting the men on their clean and smart appearance, and paying a high tribute to their fighting qualities.

August opened with the prospect of making an attack on the enemy and exercises were practised accordingly. On 6th August a Battalion reconnaissance was made which included reporting on all tracks to the front line, arranging an assembling position in "no man's land," and learning the condition of the existing wire in front of both our own and the enemy's line. The weather for some little time had been very wet, the night selected for the reconnaissance was very bright and none too suitable, and the condition of the ground was extremely muddy, making movement slow and difficult. After examining the whole situation it was recognised that any possibility of successfully attacking upon this position was out of the question. Indeed, the bad weather throughout August delayed whatever action had been contemplated by either side.

The 9th H.L.I. (The Glasgow Highlanders) were lying at Ghyvelde, and on 11th August, the 17th paid them a visit, while the Battalion football teams played a match. Another convivial day was spent on the 24th when the Battalion sports were held. The day cleared up to one of bright sunshine, and a large number of spectators enjoyed the sport. The events were continued on the following day when even a larger number of guests and spectators attended, including many Colonial soldiers, and the various events were keenly contested, both by the men of the home Battalion and those from others in the area. A good turn out of British and Belgian nurses from La Panne Hospital brightened the gathering, and at the conclusion of the sports the prizes were presented by two of the lady guests. On the Saturday following brigade sports were held under ideal conditions, the Battalion representatives winning numerous prizes.

At church parade on the 26th, the Presbyterian service was conducted in camp by the Rev. Dr. Kelman, of Free St. George's, Edinburgh, who delivered a very impressive address which was listened to with the closest attention by the men. Dr. Kelman then left to preach to another Battalion and the 17th prepared to go back to the line.

The Battalion kept up its old record of keen patrolling, and during their front line spell at the beginning of September some reconnaissance work was well carried out under conditions unusually difficult. On the night of 3rd September, 1917, 2nd Lieut. Forbes and Corpl. J. Wilson of "C" Company waded across a swamped portion which lay between the Battalion positions and a point known as Roode Poorte Farm. Coming to a point where the water was too deep for wading, Corpl. Wilson swam across and on reaching ground crawled in the direction of the enemy lines. Finding this line of approach of no use for operations, he swam back to the point where the patrol was covering his movements, and selecting another point, swam across the canal which lay to the east, opposite the farm buildings, and carried out his reconnaissance.

On the 8th, while at Wulpen, a gas attack was successfully carried through on to the enemy's lines, and on the 13th, the third anniversary of the forming of the Battalion was spent in the trenches. A telegram congratulating the Battalion on its anniversary was received from the brigadier, and a reply sent reciprocating the general's good wishes.

The enemy perpetrated a novel surprise raid, which had some of the elements of picture-house humour in it, on one of the Battalion advanced Listening Posts, and by their new device gained temporary footing in it. A strong stream of water, apparently from a hose was directed suddenly upon the men in the Listening Post from the enemy position. While the men were baffled and blinded by the rush of water, the post was bombed and the two listeners retired on the main post for support. Immediately a counter-attack was organised and led by Company Sergeant-Major Miller of "A" Company, and the post was re-established.

Orders were received on October 5th, 1917, for the relief of the 97th Infantry Brigade by the 125th Infantry Brigade. The Battalion accordingly withdrew to Coxyde that night, and on the following morning left for Adinkerke on the way to fresh fields and battles new.

The Ypres Salient

At Adinkerke, on their way to the Ypres Salient, the men were embarked on barges on October 6th, 1917, and journeyed by canal to near Rosendael where they billeted and where Lieut. Colonel J. Inglis rejoined the Battalion from leave and resumed command. They then underwent intensive training at Uxem until the 24th, when they left *en route* for the Eringham area in accordance with the forward move of the Brigade Group. The next day saw them at Rubrouck and on the next again they arrived at Broxcele where training was again entered upon and continued until November 9th.

About this period Lieut. Colonel Inglis and the adjutant, Captain F.E. Dunsmuir, were away from the Battalion making a preliminary tour of inspection of the line on the Ypres front.

On the 10th, the Battalion was once more in column of route on their way to Wormhoudt, and on the following day, to Watou to "Road Camp" in the St. Jan Ter Biezen area, where training was resumed, and this time once more within sound of the rumble of the guns. But that didn't upset the H.L.I., whose 16th and 17th Battalions met in the final of the Brigade Football Tournament, which was won in easy style, five goals to nil, by the Chamber of Commerce boys. Four days later they defeated the 32nd Divisional Supply Column in the semi-final of the Divisional Tournament, and then two days after that, meeting the 2nd Royal Inniskillen Fusiliers in the final, the 17th H.L.I. carried off the Championship, repeating their performance of the previous year against the same finalists.

On the following day the Divisional Commander addressed the Brigade, which was drawn up on the football field, and reminded the men of the sterner duties that now lay before them, and expressed the hope that they would maintain the honourable traditions associated with the name of the 97th Infantry Brigade—which, indeed, they more than maintained.

The Battalion left the camp on November 22nd for Poperinghe where they entrained to continue the journey up the line, and arriving at St. Jean Station, detrained and marched to "Irish Camp."

On the afternoon of the 23rd a start was made for the Passchendaele front line system, the route taken by the Battalion being for the greater part over the duck board walks "Mouse Trap Track," which covered ground won in the recent big push at Passchendaele. The take-over was not completed without casualties, but these were comparatively few considering the dangerous nature of the going, which was in the open over shell-pitted ground. The Battalion relieved by the 17th was the 1st Northamptonshire Battalion. During the night the 17th captured its first prisoner in this area—a corporal of the 315th Regiment. According to his statement he had been out on patrol when he lost one of his boots in the mud and in trying to find it he had strayed into our lines and been taken.

During their initial tour of the Passchendaele system much heavy work was done in converting the shell-hole defence line into trenches, and patrolling. Several casualties were reported each day and the mud was thick and sticky. On the 26th the Battalion was relieved and proceeded to Dambre Camp in the Vlamertinghe area where everybody rested and completed the preparations for the forthcoming offensive at Passchendaele.

It may be said at the outset that the element of surprise intended in the Passchendaele attack failed entirely, as the enemy were aware of the British intentions and fully prepared. In addition, the fact that the artillery barrage proper did not open until zero plus eight minutes, allowed the enemy entire freedom of action in his front posts with rifles and machine guns.

The Battalion moved into the line on the evening of December 1st in conjunction with the other Battalions of the Brigade—2nd K.O.Y.L.I.; 16th H.L.I.; 11th Border Regiment; and the 15th Lancashire Fusiliers (attached). The 16th Northumberland Fusiliers of the 96th Infantry Brigade were attached to the 97th Infantry Brigade as counter-attacking troops to be used in the event of a strong hostile counter-attack on the Brigade front. The frontage taken over by the Brigade was one of 1,850 yards approximately along the Passchendaele Ridge. There were two objectives to be taken, of which sections were detailed as the job of the 17th—a slice which included two formidable "pill-boxes" known as the "Vat and Veal Cottages."

The Battalion assembled on a frontage of 400 yards and at Zero Hour (1.55 a.m.) moved forward to the attack. Companies deployed from a two platoon frontage in snake formation—this method having been adopted owing to the shell torn nature of the ground—and advanced in four waves. "A" and "B" Companies were to capture the first objective, mopping up all occupied points in the way, including the two pill boxes, while "C" and "D" were to "leap-frog" through them, carry the next objective and consolidate.

The initial stages of the attack were successfully carried through, but the enemy—as was afterwards learned—knowing of what was on foot, waited in readiness. Suddenly he opened heavy machine gun fire upon the advancing Companies, inflicting heavy casualties which, in the dark and over the difficult ground, had the effect of splitting up the sections and creating some confusion. The officers and men of the Battalion gallantly pressed on against these odds, however, and succeeded in reaching their objective; but the enemy machine gun and rifle fire became so intense that their advanced positions were rendered humanly untenable. Our men, though forced to retire in places, established themselves in shell-hole posts, where an attempt was made to consolidate.

The artillery and machine gun barrage, though intense, had failed, owing to the enemy's fore-knowledge of the attack, to effect its purpose. His strong points were heavily garrisoned and wired and he was also found to be established in strong lines of trenches also effectively wired. The Battalion hung on all through that awful night in its isolated positions, for orders were received that the attack would be renewed in the morning, but these orders were afterwards cancelled.

From dawn onwards artillery fire slackened somewhat, but the enemy machine gunners and snipers kept up harassing fire from their well established posts against the men in their exposed and isolated posts.

It was obvious that a hostile counter-attack might be expected, and this took place about 4 p.m. on the afternoon of the 2nd, preceded by an intense artillery barrage. Owing to the terrible difficulties of their position, and the sweeping casualties inflicted, the line was forced back, but the actual enemy attack which followed his barrage was met by the rifle fire of the shattered 17th, and after the Bosches had approached within a certain distance of the posts, they broke and turned back in retreat.

Though the withdrawal of the divisional line had been almost gen-

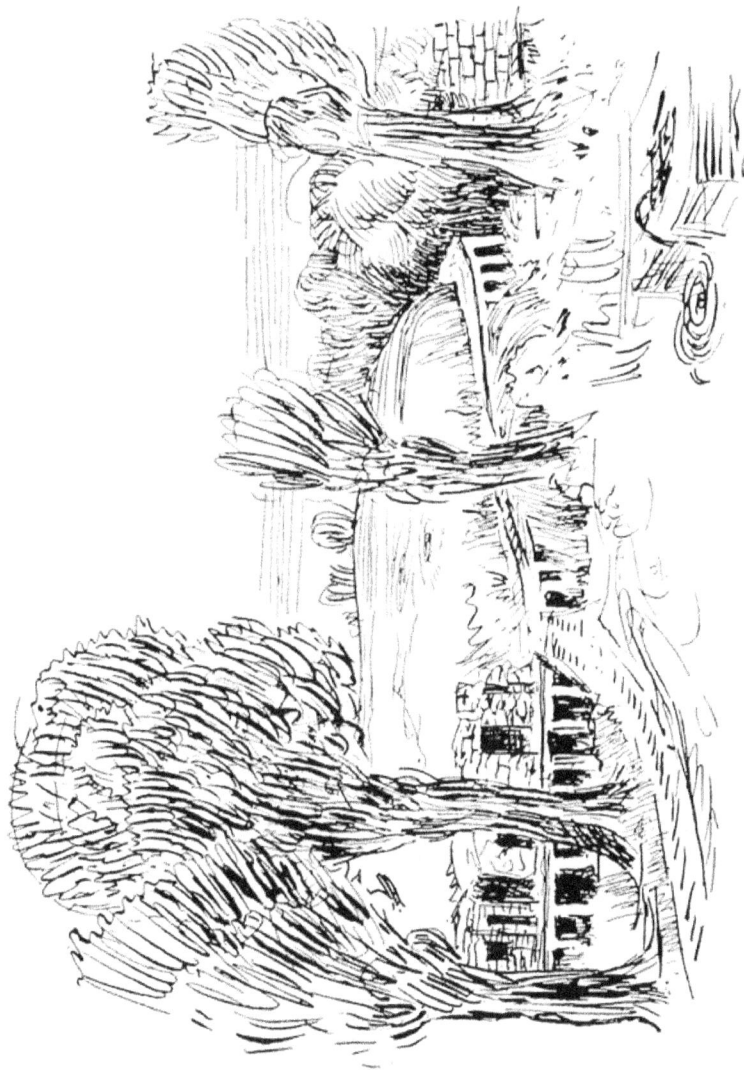

Types of Support Line Dugouts and First Aid Post.

eral, some of the Battalion posts were still hanging on to the advanced positions on the 3rd. Many wounded were lying out, suffering the most appalling rigours of war and the Battalion stretcher-bearers displayed great devotion to duty in ignoring the heavy fire while bringing them in to comparative shelter. The work at first was extremely dangerous, but later on in the day a lull occurred when it was possible to carry on this labour of mercy under less trying conditions.

And it must be recorded, as far as this battle is concerned, that from this point onward the German reversed his frequent policy and shewed respect for the Red Cross flag, only one instance of sniping taking place when one of the Battalion stretcher-bearers was shot dead while bending over a wounded comrade. Enemy stretcher-bearers were also at work and in some instances they reciprocated attentions given to their wounded, by dressing and carrying our casualties. In this way all the wounded were got in before the brigade was relieved that night. The Battalion frontage was taken over by the 5/6th Royal Scots. The relief was successfully completed and the remnants of the Battalion reached "Hilltop Farm" in the early morning, entraining later for Hospital Camp in the Vlamertinghe area.

The casualties were particularly heavy among officers and N.C.O.s, and gives trenchant evidence of their self-sacrificing gallantry in seeking by utter disregard for danger to turn a forlorn hope into victory, and by personal example and incentive to make still richer the honourable traditions of the 17th in the face of such overwhelming odds, and amidst such overaweing devastation. In this action seven officers were killed and five wounded. Of other ranks 41 were killed, 130 wounded and 13 missing.

The Battalion was organised as far as possible in its depleted condition and work and training carried on until December 10th, when once more the unit moved up the line to Hilltop Farm, N.E. of Ypres. During their stay here, Mr. Fred A. Farrell, the well-known Scottish artist, visited the 17th on a commission from the Corporation of Glasgow to execute drawings of the Glasgow Battalions and the places in which they were operating.

On December 13th they were back in the trenches. Hard winter weather had now set in, with fog, frost and water sogged ground. On the 20th the Battalion was relieved and, as far as weather is concerned, spent a typical Christmas Day when it came round, in Dambre Camp. Being in Corps Reserve, nothing in the nature of Christmas festivities could be permitted, but the gifts supplied by the Chamber of

Commerce provided seasonable fare and brought a measure of good cheer.

After a series of alarms and stand-to's, a Divisional Relief was carried through, and on December 30th the Battalion trained to Audruicq and set out on an arduous route march for the villages of Landrethun and Yeuse, where the men were happily enabled to spend a night's rest in comfortable billets, "A," "B," "C," and Headquarters in the former village, and "D" in the latter.

The last day of the year which had probably been the hardest and, as far as campaigning is concerned, the most eventful in the history of the Battalion, was passed amidst the peaceful surroundings of these villages untouched by war. The beginning of the year had seen the Battalion in the line in the Serre Sector, then had followed the memorable days of Beaumont Hamel, Honoroye, the battle of Savy and the taking of Fayet in the St. Quentin area, a well deserved period of rest at Canizy and thence by train and road into Belgium, being held in reserve for the Battle of Messines, three hard months spent in the line in the Nieuport Sector and the St. George's Sector, and then after a spell of rest—forward into Passchendaele.

The Disbandment

For some time rumours had been flitting about that certain Battalions were going to be disbanded in accordance with a programme of reorganised military establishments. Every new army unit in the B.E.F. had about this time qualms of fear that if rumours proved true the selection might fall on them. *Esprit de corps* was never stronger and the very thought of possible separations from brothers-in-arms, fell as a vague shadowy fear over the 17th because it looked very likely that the 17th, being the junior H.L.I. Battalion of the division, would be the divisional victim in any re-arrangement that might be carried out. But nothing definite was known, and the advent of New Year, 1918, brought with it a feeling of hope for the future.

The Battalion was still billeted in the peaceful villages of Landrethun and Yeuse. On the opening day of the year the ground was snow covered, rendering parades well nigh impossible, and so the men were at liberty. Preparations were eagerly pushed forward for a New Year Feast, and on the 3rd, in spite of provisioning difficulties, very complete arrangements had been successfully made considering the length of time available for providing the men with a seasonable repast on that evening. The companies sat down to a feast of roast pork—which only a few hours before had been a live pig. There was soup, haggis, plum pudding, apple dumpling, cake, cigarettes, and copious supplies of beer. The commanding officer, accompanied by Major G.R.S. Paterson, and the adjutant, visited each company in turn to wish them the compliments of the season, and the night finished with song and story.

Work and training was resumed again in earnest the next day as far as the weather conditions would permit. On the 9th of January the Battalion moved off, embussing for the forward area to operate on the 2nd Corps Line. After a cold journey in a heavy snowstorm, they arrived at Murat Camp at night and came under the command of the 35th Division.

They found the camp in very bad order and set about putting it right, meanwhile working parties were carrying on under the C.R.E. of the division. Splendid work was carried out by the Battalion during this period, despite snowstorms and blizzards, and high praise was given to the unit by the corps commander. All the Royal Engineer officers connected with the work declared they had never had better nor keener infantry parties.

On the 16th Major Morton assumed command of the Battalion during the absence of Lieut.-Colonel Inglis on leave; and on the 18th Major Morton was ordered to hospital and Major Paterson took over.

The Battalion Intelligence News Sheet, inaugurated to keep all ranks fully informed of the principal events of the day as regards the war, was circulated, but it could not hope to oust *The Outpost* as the real news vehicle of the 17th.

On the 25th of January the Battalion left Murat Camp for a camp near Woeston and came under the command of the 1st Division, and on the 27th the Battalion relieved the 10th Gloucesters in reserve in the Het Sas Sector, and carried on improving the line until the 31st of January—when the blow fell and hopes were dashed to the ground. While in Brigade Support at Houthust Forest Sector, Major Paterson was sent for by Brigadier-General C.A. Blacklock, who informed him that the re-organisation of the army necessitated the disbanding of an H.L.I. Battalion in the 32nd Division.

The Battalion selected was the junior one, the 17th. General Blacklock expressed in very generous terms his admiration for the Battalion, and for all that it had done, and expressed his sorrow and regret that so fine a unit had to be broken up, and the officers, non-com. officers and men serving in it would be drafted to other H.L.I. Battalions, which would necessitate, in many cases, the breaking up of what had been very long friendships.

Early in January, 1918, it had been decided by the War Office to adopt the three battalion per brigade system throughout the British Army, and this resulted in the disbandment of many Battalions which had seen much service abroad, and had won a name for themselves in France. Perhaps the chief Battalion in the whole army to be disbanded was the 17th Service Battalion of the Highland Light Infantry, and the disbandment of this Battalion came as a bitter blow, not only to those who were serving in the Battalion at that time, but also to those who had served in it at some time or other in the past and possibly to those who were looking forward to serving with it in the future.

Needless to say all ranks of the Battalion were deeply disappointed at the commander-in-chief's decision, which was received as a calamity. The highest traditions of the Battalion had been maintained throughout, and the *esprit de corps* and good comradeship of all ranks made the news almost unbearable.

As soon as the official notification arrived the Battalion was relieved by the First Battalion, the Dorset Regiment, and was withdrawn to Hospital Camp near Woesten where the disbanding was to be carried out. From then onwards an enormous amount of work fell on everybody, especially on the adjutant, Captain Dunsmuir, M.C., who was responsible for compiling the rolls of the different drafts, which were to proceed to the various H.L.I. Battalions in France, comprising the 10/11th, 12th, 14th, 15th, 16th, and 18th Battalions.

On the 11th of February the first draft, consisting of about seven officers and 200 other ranks marched out of camp to the tune of the pipes *en route* for the railway station at Boesinghe, where it entrained and proceeded to join the 10/11th Battalion H.L.I. Although there was much cheering as the train steamed away, yet there were many men with sad hearts at leaving the Battalion they had served in from the beginning, which had become their home in the army.

For the next few days that followed, similar drafts were sent off until the strength of the Battalion was reduced to the establishment for Headquarters with Transport. For about a week this small unit carried on, until the Transport section, under the Transport officer, Lieut. Smith, was detached, and was attached to the Division where it remained for some time until it was sent to the base for drafting. All that remained now was the Headquarters establishment, commanded by Lieut.-Colonel Inglis, D.S.O., who had returned from leave, and this establishment was sent to take over another camp which was to be run as a Divisional Reception Camp for men returning to their units from leave.

About a week later orders were received that some of the H.Q. personnel were to be drafted away, and on the next day a draft of about thirty men under R.S.M. Burns proceeded to join the 13th Entrenching Battalion. A few days later all that was left of the Battalion under Captain Dunsmuir, M.C., was drafted to the same Battalion, and Lieut.-Colonel Inglis, D.S.O., and Major Morton, who was again with the Battalion, were ordered to report to Divisional Headquarters.

All that remained now of the 17th Battalion Highland Light Infantry was the name, but that name will always remain in the minds of those who served in the Battalion, and the mere mention of it brings back happy memories of days spent both at home and abroad to those who knew it.

As William Glennie of "A" Company, writes:—

That the good old Battalion would end, we all expected, as the happy sequence of completed duty, and somehow we all imagined we would be there. In our ideal picture of the scene, George Square was clearly outlined; somehow we fancied old Hughie would order 'Officers, fall out please,' and while the ranks took the rhythmical right turn, the 'Faither' would step forward from the right of 'C' Company, give his characteristic red army salute, shake his cane and rap out 'Quick time off the parade ground' in his best Troon parade style. But we forgot the war, as too often in our ideal outlook we did.

★★★★★

'Fall out . . . the 17th Highland Light Infantry . . . .' That was at No. 6 Camp, Calais, in the chill dusk of 6th February, 1918. Back from Blighty leave, as the news spread, we took it philosophically—the old Battalion had been disbanded, and scattered to various sister battalions. Here we were, practically all the originals to the number of about 50, the sole remnants of 26 months of war, welcomed back to France for the second time, but not to the Seventeenth; orphans to be adopted by strange parents.

★★★★★

'Quick march.' The party swung slowly down the rough track between the huts. It was one of those innumerable hutted campments behind Poperinghe. At the junction of the road stood Colonel Inglis, Majors Morton and Paterson, Captain Dunsmuir and R.S.M. Kelly. It all seemed so usual, save that there was more handshaking and waving of bonnets. 'Cheerio, old chap—best of luck.' Gone, those pals of three years in camp, trench, billet and shell hole; but we never knew how great a part of our life they had become. Then in the look in each other's eyes, in the huskiness of the voice, rather than in the ill-concealed tear, came the full realisation of the undying spirit of our old Chamber of Commerce Battalion, and the certainty that the death of the Battalion had bequeathed to us the Living Soul of the Seventeenth.

The Spirit of the Battalion

A corporate body is always a great mystery. Before very long it always develops a spirit which is something more than the sum of the individual spirits which compose it. And no man can quite say how it comes into existence. It may be a greater spirit than that of any individual. Sometimes it is not so great as that of its members.

And Battalions are no exception to this rule. Each brings forth a spirit, and by that spirit the members are henceforth profoundly influenced. It is not the spirit of the colonel, or of any particular member. It is the spirit of the Battalion, something compounded by the subtle alchemies of the spiritual world out of the individual souls of officers and privates alike.

Of the spirit of the 17th H.L.I. it may at once be said that the outstanding characteristic was high-hearted youth. Most of the members of the Battalion were young, but the Battalion itself had the qualities of youth more truly than any of them. It was essentially gay. It did its work to the accompaniment of a fine hilarity. It could laugh even on the eve of battle. It could even be uproarious and exuberant as only the really young can.

And yet it was very efficient youth. To a man these soldiers took their work seriously, and because they brought to it a fine quality of intelligence, the Battalion rose to efficiency with astonishing rapidity. Many men read eagerly in text books about training and tactics and so forth, and the Battalion from end to end was intolerant of slovenliness. If it resembled a young man, it was a young man who meant business.

MAJOR THE REV. A. HERBERT GRAY.

CHURCH PARADE—PREES HEATH CAMP.

In the Line after the Route March

The Wash-up.

Advancing to the Attack.

Church Parade.

Getting Stuck.

Defending the Hill.

Cooking Dept.

VARIOUS PHASES OF BATTALION TRAINING.

It was also very gifted youth. Its athletic record speaks for itself, as does also its military record. But other gifts were lavished upon it. It knew and loved good literature. It had numbers of trained singers and musicians. It had dramatic possibilities in it. It knew much of science and mechanics. That young thing which we call the 17th H.L.I. in fact loved life, and every side of life. It throbbed with energy of body, mind, and spirit. It tingled with many sided vitality.

But above all, it was loveable youth. Few bodies of soldiers have ever so fully won the affections of towns and country districts. It has left a mark of its own on Troon, Prees Heath, Wensley, Sheffield, and Codford. People hurried out to see the column go by, and after it was gone the hearts of men and women were happier because of it. It came to have a place in the lives of thousands, and they all thought of it with affection. As we look back on it now it lives with us as a silver memory,—something belonging to the world of sunshine and laughter, of beauty and of courage. The West of Scotland gave of its best to make up that whole, and while it lived it made a place for itself in the hearts of the West, which is secure for all time.

Its career was short, but its immortality is safe.

It is good to have known it. And though tragedy unspeakable dogged its footsteps, and broke its life in this world, it lives and will always live gloriously in the hearts and memories of uncounted men and women who believe more in humanity, and perhaps even believe more in God because of the "Seventeenth."

"Co-operation"

One of the most outstanding and important things taught in military text books is the value of striving to obtain "co-operation of all arms." That is to say, the more sympathy, good comradeship and understanding that exists between infantry and artillery and cavalry and tanks and air force people and so on, the more efficient each of these various arms becomes to carry out its respective duties. Knowledge of the general tactical principles under which each arm operates, and personal acquaintanceship with the various officers and men of such other units, all tend to cement combined operations into one smooth working whole for the pleasant efficiency of the combinations concerned and for the better (or worse!) confusion of the enemy.

Such co-operation was an ideal often aimed at, but only too seldom actually accomplished. It required the best of officers and men to attain that perfect co-operation through understanding, which does not either fall short of or over reach the mark.

The following notes written by Major C.E. Lawder, late commanding "A" Battery of the 168th Brigade, 32nd Division, Royal Field Artillery, reveals how smoothly things ran in that all important section of co-operation—that between Infantry and Artillery. In the eyes of those accustomed to military affairs the following statements will likely be recognised as perhaps the finest tribute that could be paid to the 17th H.L.I., for it is not so much an item of direct praise, as a sure indication of the high quality of efficiency attained by all ranks of the Battalion, not to mention the pleasant reflection given of "good humoured gentlemen." The 17th was ever proud to serve with the gunners of the 168th Brigade, whose fine shooting inspired confidence and courage:—

We first met the famous 17th H.L.I. about New Year, 1916, in the La Boiselle Sector and much concern as to the pronunciation of the Scottish names given to the trenches was felt by my Yorkshire gunners—Sauchiehall Street in particular defeated them. They wished the Jocks would use Christian Huddersfield names! All my officers were much impressed by the great kindness and hospitality shown them by the 17th H.L.I. Messes when liaison Officer with the Infantry or when going round the front line, which we did constantly, myself as Battery Commander every third day, and the subalterns daily—all to try and get suggestions to better strafe the Boche and to show the Jocks that the gunners wanted to share the pleasures of the front line with our splendid Infantry.

The 17th were commonly known as the Raiders, and most excellent they were at the job—the Hun had a holy horror of the men from Glasgow. I well remember a chat after a good raid with the big drummer and a little corporal of the H.L.I. Both had greatly distinguished themselves and they asked me not to question them as to details of the raid, as some very dirty work took place across the way! I expect it did from the look in their eye and the happy way they handled their clubs.

A great *entente cordiale* existed between my battery and the regiment and this was referred to by Major-General Budworth, C.R.A., 4th Army, at the Conference at Flixecourt before July 1st, 1916. All the gunners at the gun position, then in the Orchard of Martinsart, sent in a signed petition to be allowed to have the honour of going over the top with the 17th in their next raid. The 17th returned the compliment by Major W. Paul and about 20 raiders coming up to the guns from Rest billets and carrying ammunition for us all night while we were covering another regiment's raid. I got Major Paul on the firing seat of one of the guns and some of the men at other guns. They did a lot of firing but did not enjoy it. They all preferred the Infantry!

The 17th were badly cut up on 1st July, 1916, and my men were much concerned about them. We were all greatly relieved to hear that both Col. Morton and Major Paul were not among the casualties. Some of the Officers will doubtless remember a cheery *Entente* Dinner at Bouzincourt—Cocktails by our adjutant, Lobsters and Rouen Ducks are still fresh in my memory. The Division moved up north to the Hulluch Sector after the Somme July Battle. We were put to another Division for a short time, and then our own Infantry turned up. It was cheery meeting our old friends again, but many familiar names and faces were, sad to say, missing.

We had a very safe and nice gun position on a peninsula in a marsh at Annieguin. This we made into a very smart and show position—lots of "spit and polish." We had many visitors from the 17th and a lot of their men used to come and bathe with ours. We fixed up a regular bathing pool with springboard complete. All this was under cover of trees and shrubs and quite out of sight of the Hun. I remember two of the H.L.I. being pulled from or being stabbed in, a sap in No Man's Land near the famous Brickstacks. We all wanted to have a Raid at once in revenge. I forget whether it came off. Shooting here was difficult, as the trenches were so close together, and very difficult to observe fire.

Very different was the supply of ammunition in mid and late 1916 to early in the year. It was a horrible feeling for a Battery when asked to shoot and help the poor old Infantry, to have to refuse for lack of shells. At the Brickstacks we used to often fire—almost daily—from 150 to 350 rounds Agressive Action on Hun Tender Spots. It was then that we could retaliate about 50 to 1 if they were sufficiently "agressed" to fire back. That kept the line—our side (!)—quiet.

We all moved down in October, 1916, to the Ancre show, and a horrible wet march it was. We separated for a bit, the Battery going to the Scottish 51st Division. We were then rejoined by our own Infantry at Beaumont Hamel. I got smashed up and was evacuated home, and just after, my best officer, Lieut. H.W. Ainley was burned to death at the Wagon Line. He was a splendid fellow and very well known to the 17th.

Officers and men of both Units were always together and better feeling between them could not exist. It was a great honour to know the 17th and we gloried in being the battery to cover them at the P. of E. in a raid.

[The P. of E. is the Point of Entry, necessitating very accurate gunlaying, timing, and strict adherence to the barrage programme.]

"THE OUTPOST" STAFF ON ACTIVE SERVICE.

THE ORIGINAL EDITORIAL STAFF. SGT. FERGUSON,
THE LATE SGT. REITH AND PTE. HUTCHESON.

"The Outpost"

One of the most outstanding activities of the Battalion was the production of a periodical which combined a considerable high level of artistic and literary excellence with a racy narrative of Battalion news and *personalia*. This regimental magazine of the 17th H.L.I. was conceived in 1914, though actually founded early in 1915, and from that time, throughout all the rigours of work at home—and the extraordinary difficulties of operations in the Field, *The Outpost* was produced, and well produced. Perhaps more than anything, the standard and record of this production, and its acceptance and success, both within the unit and with an ever growing general public, reflects the intellectual level of those who composed the Battalion. In an appreciation which appeared in *The Glasgow News* in June, 1919, on the occasion of the completion of the seventh volume, it is remarked—

Nursed in its early youth by an editorial staff that was not without experience, it proved a lusty infant, and as the years went on it gained in strength.

In a sort of valedictory—for the magazine will still be published annually by the Seventeen Club—the editor sings its praises. He has every right to pitch them on a high key. He points out that the paper has always been welcomed and appreciated in many homes (yes, even in Buckingham Palace), and in training camps, hospitals, rest camps, lonely dugouts, and soaking trenches, as well as in the scorching East and amid Arctic snows. Wherever old members have gone at duty's call, their magazine has followed, and has interested and cheered with its articles and illustrations of the lighter side of Army life.

Lately a noted writer on military topics, an English officer of high rank, in giving a most appreciative criticism of *The Outpost*, said—'It is only your dour, determined Scotsmen who could manage to "carry-on" such a paper under the tremendous handicaps of active service, and the result has been unquestionably the finest literary and artistic venture in battalion magazines that the war has produced.'

In a note concerning those who originated and inspired this war publication—unique in its continued success—Mr. J. M'Kechnie, whose name is intimately associated with its success, says—

The credit of the original idea of publishing a Battalion Magazine belongs to Lieut. J. Kelly—our first R.S.M. Early in January, 1915, he called a meeting at which the journalistic machinery was set in motion. The appointment of the late Mr. Steven D. Reith as editor assured the success of the venture, for under his able and enthusiastic direction, *The Outpost* from the first number reached a standard hitherto unapproached in British military publications. From month to month it supplied a bright literary and artistic reflection of the chief events in the life of the Battalion, and the editorial aimed at giving a lead to the more serious thought of its readers.

Throughout its active service career *The Outpost* was edited by the following:—The late Mr. Steven D. Reith, Mr. J.L. Hardie, Mr. J. M'Kechnie, and Mr. W. Glennie. Mr. W. J.F. Hutcheson performed the duties of Home Editor until November, 1917, when he handed on the torch to Mr. Frank K. Pickles, who acted as Editor during the last year.

Copies and volumes of *The Outpost* will remain among the most cherished keepsakes of all members of the Battalion, and a complete set of all numbers of the production is being carefully and jealously preserved in the archives of the Glasgow Chamber of Commerce. There its pages will rank with the greatest achievements of industrial and commercial affairs as evidence of the judgment, humour, poetry, and doggedness of a Battalion so intimately bound up in the traditions of a great house, and indeed, also reflective of the traditions of Scottish industrialism, whose eminence is the manifestation of those very elements of balanced judgment and perseverance, coupled with that saving humour and imagination which has marked alike its progress in the markets of the world no less than in the fields of war.

THE LATE STEVEN D. REITH,
D.C.M.

LCE.-CORPL. F.K. PICKLES.

MARGUS—THE MASCOT.

ONE OF THE BATTALION RUGBY FOOTBALL TEAMS.

Sport of the Battalion

The achievements of the Seventeenth in the field of fire cannot be dissociated from their experiences in the field of sport. The exploits of the Battalion in football, cross-country running, and boxing—revealing as they did the elements of challenge, perseverance, cheerfulness in defeat, and also the power to win honours to their name—have their grand reflex in the more grim and arduous experiences through which the Battalion was called to pass.

In October, 1915, the Battalion won divisional honours in cross-country running. The winning of the cup and medals in an event in which a thousand runners took part was no small feat.

In the world of "rugger" the Battalion's career was one triumphal march, but the end accomplished cannot be summed up in figures, adverse or the reverse. As for "soccer" the successive achievements of the Battalion are recorded in every number of *The Outpost*. Minor struggles and conquests are recalled and rejoiced in, but the glory of carrying off another Divisional Cup will never be forgotten by those who witnessed the fray. Progress to the final of the event was not easy, and the final was a particularly hard fought game, and though the Battalion won, it was felt that equal honours were due to the vanquished for their good play and sportsmanship.

In the boxing world, the name of Corporal George Barrie, will be ever green in the memory of all Seventeenth men; and the honour brought to the Battalion by his pupil, Pte. Cushley, in winning two Divisional Cups for boxing, can be looked upon as a fitting tribute to Barrie, the man who played the game even unto death.

Altogether the Seventeenth has much to be proud of in its athletic record, and in future days when those of the Battalion sit round and tell of the things which are theirs, which they won also at great cost, their prowess in the field will not be among the least; for it played no insignificant part in the making of the Battalion which, although disbanded, has remained, both in name and in comradeship, still the Seventeenth.

The R.S.M.

Any history of the "Seventeenth" would be incomplete without a passing reference to James Kelly.

Chosen at the inception of the Battalion out of a large number of applicants, and appointed regimental sergeant major, his selection was amply justified by results. He had seen much service in The Royal Scots, and active service in South Africa, where he was colour-sergeant of his company and where he gained the D.C.M.

A man of commanding appearance, always very smartly turned out, he set a fine example to all ranks and speedily infused the real military spirit into the rank and file. During training at home and on service in France he did splendid work, and to him is due in no small measure the high standard of efficiency and discipline maintained in the Battalion. In manner somewhat brusque, but of a tender heart withal, he was the friend and confidant of nearly all the officers, N.C.O.s and men, and when off parade the best of good fellows.

David S. Morton,
Lieut.-Colonel.

A Remembrance

Do you hear it, all of you, and remember. Listen!

"Markers outwards turn. Quick march."

"Up, number four. Look sharp. That'll do."

"Markers, steadi-i-i-i——."

"Right turn."

"Fall in." And then the final great roar of—

"Stop all that yammering." And how quickly it stopped, too.

Do you remember it, and who said it? Of course you do, just as clearly as I myself do. You remember those early mornings, too. The sleepy chatter stilled in an instant to silence. And all those other days, too, when custom had made it imperative on all parades, it was part of us and our ceremonial.

The repeating of it to ourselves conjures up the history of those never-to-be-forgotten days and carries back our spirits to commune with all those gone before us.

I say it to myself often now just to bring before me those wonderful memories. I have heard it on the sea front at Troon; on the Hills of Dundonald; at Prees Heath, in the lovely woodlands and parks of England; on the moors of Yorkshire; at Sheffield. It has sounded over the vast spaces of Salisbury Plain, and in France and Flanders, where all it stands for was so wonderfully justified and upheld, calling up that wonderful spirit and special discipline. That was the dear old Seventeenth.

LIEUT. AND Q.-M. (FORMERLY
REGIMENTAL SERGEANT MAJOR)
JAMES KELLY.

MRS. DAVID S. MORTON
CONVENER OF THE COMFORTS
COMMITTEE.

The Comforts Committee

On the Battalion embarking for active service, the Battalion Committee suggested that a Ladies' Committee be formed to carry out the supply of comforts which would tend to alleviate the hardships of the battle line. The members of the Chamber provided funds in a most generous manner, and the following ladies consented to form a Ladies' Committee:—Mrs. D.S. Morton (Convener), Lady M'Innes Shaw, Mrs. J.M. Mitchell, Mrs. R.A. Murray, Mrs. W.J. Paul, Mrs. W.F. Russell, Mrs. John Reid, Mrs. Albert A. Smith, and Miss G.D. Young.

Miss G.D. Young acted as secretary and at a later stage she was succeeded by Miss M.E. M'Clymont of the staff of the Chamber. The relatives of the men of the Battalion were notified of the formation of the Comforts Committee, and were invited to assist in knitting articles, the wool for which in most cases, was supplied by the Committee. With this help, and by the industry of the Ladies' Committee, a very large quantity of shirts, socks, helmets, scarfs, gloves, etc., was sent abroad.

The conditions under which the men were fighting was always wisely considered, and for trench dug-outs and cellar billets, a regular supply of candles was forwarded by the Committee. Christmas presents were also sent overseas for each man. Provision was made for the time when the Battalion was out of line for rest, and a supply of weekly and monthly periodicals was regularly despatched. Needless to say, all these were very acceptable.

While thanks are due to all the members of the Ladies' Committee, it must be placed on record that Mrs. Morton, as convener, rendered invaluable services and it is universally recognised that to her indefatigable labours the men in France owed much.

Memorial Service in Glasgow

A Memorial Service in honour of the officers, non-commissioned officers and men of the 17th Highland Light Infantry, who fell in the battle of the Somme and elsewhere was held at Glasgow Cathedral, on July 8th, 1917. Fully 1,200 people were present, and many soldiers of all ranks were among the congregation, including a number of wounded men belonging to the Battalion. The "Dead March in Saul" was played at the commencement, and the service was most impressive throughout. The preacher was the Rev. A. Herbert Gray, one time chaplain of the Battalion, and the service included the anthem, "What are these?" sung by the choir.

Preaching from the text—"We also are compassed about with so great a cloud of witnesses," Mr. Gray said: "It must not be to mere mourning that we give ourselves this afternoon. We are met to recall a very great page in the history of our city and district. In the year 1916, the hundreds of young men of whom we are thinking dared to die in a great cause. Young, strong, and free, full of high hopes and great purpose, in love with life, and in a hundred ways fitted for mastery in it, they yet consented to deal with death.

"A hundred other ambitions had flushed their hearts, but because humanity called they laid them all aside and went to the great war. No such life was their choice, but because it was their destiny they accepted it with a smile. No compulsion save that of honour constrained them. They were recruited simply by conscience and the claims of humanity. They made one of the finest Battalions that ever left these shores, for some of the very best of the rising generation were in their ranks. And though they were not soldiers by profession they proved themselves worthy of a regiment that has traditions of honour as old as the British Army.

"Wherefore, here in God's House, we may well first of all rejoice concerning them, and give thanks to God who has put so great a spirit into man. Though tears be in our hearts we must not fail to be proud and thankful—proud because they were our brothers, and thankful because they finished their course in faith."

After mentioning the subject of a suitable memorial, and suggesting that there could be nothing more worthy than the monument of a Britain turned to God, the preacher concluded with the following impressive words:—

From a hundred lonely graves in that foreign land—from the spots where they fell, and which now are sacred spots for us— our dead are asking us when we mean to erect that monument. From trench and shell hole where death found them, their voices call—young, musical voices, the voices of boys still in their teens, the voices of martyrs on life's threshold. Scarce a wind can blow that will not waft to you these voices. And they ask a better Britain as their monument. They ask it of you and me. Shall we not go from this place resolved to build it?

The Club

Much has been written, and many discussions have arisen concerning the good-fellowship and camaraderie which exists among the survivors of the 17th H.L.I., and able pens will express the high ideals aimed at, and the strong determination in the minds of those remnants to establish "The Club" on a basis good and sound. Since the inauguration of the Battalion in September, 1914, there has been a predominating feeling that such an institution should be made.

Since the first batch of men arrived in Glasgow from France arrangements were made which facilitated meeting daily in Craig's Smoke Room in Gordon Street—the arrangement still holds good. Any forenoon the boys may be found over their coffee and incidentally discussing the chance of one day, in the near future, having a "nook" of their own. The object of having such a place is to afford such privacy as premises of their own would give, in order to have uninterrupted meetings, business or pleasure, as the occasion demanded.

One great object of the Club is to establish the Benevolent Fund of the Battalion on a sound financial basis, so as to be in a position to deal with necessitous cases connected with the 17th Battalion, and it is thought that this is the only way. It is intended that the Club should be self-supporting, and assistance is hoped for, morally and financially, of all those who are interested in the affairs appertaining to the old Battalion.

A committee to carry on the good work has been formed, and includes Colonel Morton, Major Young, with Messrs. Ritchie, Tilley, Corbett and M'Andrew from the various Companies, along with Mr. J.W. Arthur on the Benevolent Fund Committee, as representing the Chamber of Commerce. This committee will report progress to a general meeting, at which it is hoped to decide what steps may be taken to acquire a working capital. It is possible that a voluntary subscription list may be opened, and it is hoped that the opportunity may be given to help the worthy project of thus forming a memorial to those who have fallen in the great cause.

No better monument of love and good-fellowship could be thought of than to give a helping hand in the hour of need, and, to provide towards a comfortable home for those who are left to enjoy it.

"E" Company

At the beginning of January, 1915, the 17th H.L.I. had recruited its full war strength, and the authorities decreed that a Reserve Company should be formed. This became "E" Company, and was trained as a unit of the Battalion at Troon, until the 17th left for England. On May 13th, 1915, it was transferred to Gailes, and became a unit of the 19th Reserve Battalion, Lieut.-Colonel Auld being in command. Under his training, the Company, as well as the Battalion, reached a high standard of efficiency. After being inspected by Brigadier-General Cockburn on the 28th September, 1916, a draft of 101 N.C.O.s and men was sent to join the 17th H.L.I. at Codford. What was left of "E" Coy. entrained on 26th October, 1915, at Gailes for Ripon. The men were billeted in excellent huts in the South Camp of that quaint old cathedral town, where route marches took place and many excursions were made to many of the interesting towns and places of interest.

When the 17th embarked for France, some details left behind arrived from Codford on 15th December, 1915, and brought back many old friends and highly efficient instructors. Later on Viscount French paid a visit of inspection to the Ripon area, and the 19th H.L.I. formed part of the Guard of Honour on that occasion.

After Ripon came Montrose, and although connected with the Battalion's history only in a small way, the period from 25th April, 1916, to 12th June, 1917, is nevertheless well worthy of mention. Montrose with its lovely beaches and pleasant surroundings, forms one of the happiest memories of those who found themselves part of the 19th H.L.I. during its sojourn there.

1916-17 was a trying time in the life of the Reserve Battalion. Training was concentrated to an unheard-of degree—a recruit being allowed nine short weeks before he found himself on Embarkation Leave. Drafts were required by the dozen, both for the Western

LIEUT.-COLONEL W. AULD, V.D.

The late Lt.-Col. William Herbert Anderson, V.C.

The late Sergt. J. Y. Turnbull, V.C.

Front (for which the Somme and Beaumont Hamel Offensives were chiefly responsible) and for the Eastern Front. Then there was the trying coastguard work with its trench-digging excursions to Lunan Bay—work which probably helped to avert a danger not so remote as we then imagined.

"E" Company had a fair share of all these worries, and its able commander, Captain F.D. Morton, was kept busy choosing drafts, arranging programmes, and working out tactical schemes.

Major W.H. Anderson, who afterwards became lieut.-colonel, and was awarded the V.C. after his lamented death, did much for the good of the Battalion; and the Soldiers' Home, run by Mrs. Anderson, and Mrs. Auld, proved of great advantage to the men. This period marked the extinction of "E" Company, as representing the 17th. Draft after draft had robbed it of its original appearance, and when on 1st September, 1916, the 19th became the 78th Training Reserve Battalion, it lost all semblance of its former self, and may be said to have had an inglorious end to a short but useful life.

Battalion Honour

Extract from *The London Gazette*, dated 26/5/16.

The following is extracted from Sir Douglas Haig's Despatch, dated 19/5/16:—

8.—While many other units have done excellent work during the period under review, the following have been brought to my notice for good work in carrying out or repelling local attacks and raids—

17th (Service) Battalion Highland Light Infantry.

Victoria Cross

†Lieut.-Colonel W.H. Anderson, formerly Captain "C" Company. Gained while serving with 12th Battalion H.L.I.

†15888 Sergeant J.Y. Turnbull. *Gazette* dated 25/12/16.

The following is the extract from *The London Gazette* of 3rd May, 1918, intimating the award of the Victoria Cross:—

T. Maj. (A. Lt.-Col.) William Herbert Anderson, late H.L.I. For most conspicuous bravery, determination, and gallant leading of his command. The enemy attacked on the right of the Battalion frontage, and succeeded in penetrating the wood held by our men. Owing to successive lines of the enemy following on closely there was the gravest danger that the flank of the whole position would be turned. Grasping the seriousness of the situation, Colonel Anderson made his way across the open in full view of the enemy now holding the wood on the right, and after much effort succeeded in gathering the remainder of the two right companies. He personally led the counter attack, and drove the enemy from the wood, capturing 12 ma-

---

† Since deceased.

chine guns and 70 prisoners, and restoring the original line. His conduct in leading the charge was quite fearless, and his most splendid example was the means of rallying and inspiring the men during a most critical hour.

Later on in the same day the enemy had penetrated to within 300 yards of the village, and were holding a timber yard in force. Colonel Anderson re-organised his men after they had been driven in, and brought them forward to a position of readiness for a counter-attack. He led the attack in person, and throughout showed the utmost disregard for his own safety. The counter-attack drove the enemy from his position, but resulted in this very gallant officer losing his life. He died fighting within the enemy's lines, setting a magnificent example to all who were privileged to serve under him.

Among the first to join the 17th H.L.I. was Captain W.H. Anderson, a man widely known and highly respected in Glasgow social and business circles. He was with the Battalion during most of its training at Gailes and Troon, and before embarking for Service in France was gazetted as Major in the 19th H.L.I. He served with the same rank in the East Surreys till invalided home in March, 1917. On his return to France he was transferred to an H.L.I. Battalion, becoming Lieut.-Colonel, and shortly afterwards was killed in an attack at the head of his men of the 12th H.L.I. as recorded above.

Sergeant James Y. Turnbull, V.C.

It has been said of James Turnbull that he began to win his V.C. at Troon. He was a born leader, and always a fearless champion of fairplay. He towered above the average man in strength of character as he did in stature, and he was always the same unassuming and genial "Jimmy." He was a fitting embodiment of the ideals of the Seventeenth. A big man for a big occasion—and the big occasion came along on the 1st of July, 1916.

The position of the Battalion was that of a wedge driven against the iron of impregnability, and the driving force suddenly withdrawn. At the thin end of the wedge Sergeant Turnbull, with a handful of men, performed prodigies of valour. From three sides enemy machine guns swept the position, snipers took deadly toll, and bombing attacks were constantly launched. Exposure meant almost certain death. The position was not only desperate; it was hopeless. Yet it was necessary to hold on till nightfall. It was a *man's* job, and Turnbull filled the bill.

He shouldered the responsibility as only a strong man could; and he organised the defence. He had to take countless risks, and was always where the fighting was fiercest. He was the indomitable leader and inspiring example. Wounded, he carried on till his last risk was taken, and he met a soldier's death towards the end of that fateful summer day.

Of a band of heroes he was the beloved leader and super-hero.

Honours Gained by Officers and Others while Serving with the Battalion.

Extract from *The London Gazette*, dated 3/6/16.

To be additional member of the Third Class or Companion of the Most Distinguished Order of Saint Michael and Saint George.

Lieut.-Colonel D.S. Morton, V.D.

Military Cross.

	Date of Gazette
†Lieut. A. J. Begg,	30/05/16
2nd Lieut J. L. Brodie,	26/05/17
†2nd Lieut. J. N. Carpenter,	30/05/16
Lieut. A. N. Drsydale,	13/02/17
Capt. F. E. Dunsmuir,	01/01/18
Lieut. J. L. M'Connell,	17/09/17
2nd Lieut. W. M. Martin,	26/05/17
Major G. R. S. Paterson,	26/09/16
†Capt. Jas. Russell,	01/01/17
Capt. J. D. Russell,	26/05/17
2nd Lieut. D. G. Thorburn,	18/06/17
15214 R.Q.-M.S. W. Dunsmore,	01/01/17
15394 C.S.M. A. Millar,	06/04/18

Mentioned in Despatches.

The London Gazette, dated 15/6/16.
    Lieut.-Colonel D.S. Morton, V.D.
    15205 Regt. S.M. J. Kelly.

The London Gazette, dated 4/1/17.
    †Capt. J.S. Marr.

The London Gazette, dated 25/5/17

---

†Since deceased.

2nd Lieut. F.E. Dunsmuir.
16109 Sergt. W. Wallace.

The London Gazette, dated 21/12/17.
Major G.R.S. Paterson, M.C.
15510 Sergt. J.C. Bruce.
16084 Sergt. Y. Gilbert.
16085 Pte. W. Parker.

DISTINGUISHED CONDUCT MEDAL.

15849 Sergt. W. Fraser,	01/01/18
2797 Sergt. F. Leiper,	13/02/17
15866 C.S.M. W. Mather,	01/01/17
115507 C.S.M. S. D. Reith,	30/05/16

BAR TO MILITARY MEDAL.

†2997 Sergt. N. Connor, M.M.

MILITARY MEDAL.

†123053 Pte. G. S. Anderson,	26/05/17
15255 Cpl. J. Chapman,	10/11/16
†2997 Sergt. N. Connor,	16/02/17
16004 Pte. J. K. Deans,	16/02/17
15937 L.-Sergt. W. Dickson,	17/09/17
15937 Cpl. F. Farnell,	17/09/17
15582 L.-Cpl. A. V. Follett,	17/09/17
40899 Pte. A. B. Forrest,	17/09/17
15581 Pte. C. N. Fraser,	16/02/17
16084 Sergt. Y. Gilbert,	16/02/17
2727 L.-Cpl. W. Glennie,	26/05/17
41046 Pte. J. Hogg,	26/05/17
2744 Pte. J. C. Hunter,	20/10/16
9808 Sergt. J. Johnstone,	26/05/17
2797 Pte. F. Leiper,	03/06/16
15748 Sergt. F. M. M'Gregor,	16/02/17
†15720 Pte. D. Macintosh,	03/06/16
15363 Pte. A. G. M'Nair,	10/11/16
†15677 Sergt. J. Maxwell,	16/02/17
†16146 Sergt. R. Milligan,	29/08/17
†15964 Sergt. J. Osborne,	16/02/17
27267 L.-Cpl. J. Pearson,	26/05/17

† Since deceased.

2725 L.-Sergt. J. Ramage,	26/05/17
41198 Pte. E. Reddington,	26/05/17
15415 Sergt. T. Ritchie,	20/10/16
15775 Sergt. J. Roberts,	16/02/17
28057 L.-Cpl. P. Robertson,	26/05/17
43268 Pte. T. Scott,	16/02/17
13688 Pte. R. J. Slowey,	16/02/17
42378 Pte. P. Smith,	26/05/17
15956 C.Q.M.S. W. Stewart,	16/02/17
†15458 Sergt. H. G. Taylor,	03/06/16
16149 Cpl. H. Thorburn,	26/05/17
41607 Pte. D. Turnbull,	18/06/17
15938 Sergt. A. G. Watson,	16/02/17
15818 Pte. R. M. Watson,	16/02/17
40530 Pte. J. Watt,	26/04/17
353079 Pte. F. S. Willder,	17/09/17

MERITORIOUS SERVICE MEDAL.

15544 Sergt. M. Cullen.
16064 L.-Cpl. J. Hutton, att. IV. Corps.
15710 L.-Cpl. J. A. M'Dougall, 32nd Division.
16169 Sergt. J. F. Sinclair, 97th Brigade.

BELGIAN CROIX DE GUERRE.

15310 C.S.M. G. Hirst.
16109 C.Q.M.S. W. Wallace.

HONOURS GAINED BY ORIGINAL MEMBERS OF THE BATTALION
AFTER BEING TRANSFERRED TO OTHER UNITS.

DISTINGUISHED SERVICE ORDER.

Major G.R.S. Paterson, 5th K.O.S.B.,
formerly Major 17th H.L.I.

Capt. J.D. Young, 10th A. & S. Highlanders,
formerly 2916 Pte. "B" Coy.

BAR TO MILITARY CROSS.

Lieut. J. Callan, M.C., 12th H.L.I.,
formerly 15527 L.-Cpl., "A" Coy.

Capt. A.W. Donald, M.C., 252 Coy. R.E.,
formerly 15200 L.-Cpl. "B" Coy.

---

† Since deceased.

†2nd Lieut. C.B. Meadows, M.C,
King's Own Royal Lancashire Regiment,
formerly 23015 Pte. "C" Coy.

Lieut. R. Anderson, 13th Battalion Tank Corps,
formerly 15832 Sergeant "A" Coy.

Lieut. H.T. Baird, 447th Coy. R.E.,
formerly 15509 Pte. "A" Coy.

2nd Lieut. A. Brown, A. & S. Highlanders,
formerly 16187 Pte. "C" Coy.

Lieut. J. Callan, 12th H.L.I.,
formerly 15527 L.-Cpl. "A" Coy.

Lieut. S. Campbell, 12th H.L.I.,
formerly 15982 Pte. "C" Coy.

Lieut. J.H. Carswell,
1st Northumberland Fusiliers,
formerly 2708 L.-Cpl. "B" Coy.

Captain A.W. Donald, 252nd Coy. R.E.,
formerly 15200 L.-Cpl. "B" Coy.

2nd Lieut. A.G. Drummond, 6th Black Watch,
formerly 23011 Pte. "A" Coy.

2nd Lieut. H.C. Davie,
1/8th Battalion Scottish Rifles,
formerly 15561 L.-Cpl. "C" Coy.

Lieut. A.F. Ferguson, H.L.I., attached R.A.F.,
formerly 15282 C.Q.M.S. "A" Coy.

†2nd Lieut. E.L. Garvie,
9th H.L.I. (Glasgow Highlanders),
formerly 2956 Pte. "B" Coy.

Lieut. H.P. Haddow, King's Royal Rifle Corps,
formerly 15854 L.-Cpl. "A" Coy.

†Captain J.M. Hamilton, Lancashire Fusiliers,
formerly 2783 Pte. "B" Coy.

Lieut. H. Henderson, Liverpool Scottish,
formerly 16182 Sergt. "C" Coy.

2nd Lieut. J.F. Holmes, 9th Scottish Rifles,
formerly 15856 Pte. "C" Coy.

† Since deceased.

Lieut. J.L. Jack, Machine Gun Corps,
formerly 2843 Pte. "C" Coy.

Lieut. S.F. Johnstone, Durham Light Infantry,
formerly 15323 Cpl. "C" Coy.

2nd Lieut. H.W. Jordon,
19th Durham Light Infantry,
formerly 2698 L.-Cpl. "C" Coy.

Staff-Capt. T.P. Locking, General List,
formerly 15657 Sergt. "B" Coy.

2nd Lieut. R. Love, 222nd Coy. R.E.,
formerly 15336 Pte. "A" Coy.

Capt. F.M. M'Gregor, M.M., Northants Regiment,
formerly 15748 Act.-C.S.M. "C" Coy.

†2nd Lieut. C.B. Meadows,
King's Own Royal Lancashire Regiment,
formerly 23015 Pte. "C" Coy.

Lieut. A.A. Miller,
9th H.L.I. (Glasgow Highlanders),
formerly 15680 Pte. "B" Coy.

†Lieut. J. Miller, 7th A. & S. Highlanders,
formerly 2970 Pte. A. & S.H. Cy.

Capt. F.D. Morton, 25th Royal Fusiliers,
formerly Lieut. "C" Coy.

Sub-Lieut. T.I. Morton,
"Anson" Battalion, R.N. Division,
formerly 15693 "C" Coy.

Capt. J.D. Young, 10th A. & S. Highlanders,
formerly 2916 Pte. "B" Coy.

MEMBER OF THE ORDER OF THE BRITISH EMPIRE.

Lieut. W. Hogg, Intelligence Corps,
formerly 15629 Cpl. "B" Coy.

DISTINGUISHED CONDUCT MEDAL.

34834 Sergt. T. Garmory,
8th York and Lancaster Regiment,
formerly 2985 Pte. "D" Coy.

---

†Since deceased.

†22355 Sergt. J.A. Wark, Machine Gun Corps,
formerly 15461 Pte. "B" Coy.

MILITARY MEDAL.

16018 Pte. R. Hood, 2nd Battn. H.L.I.,
formerly "D" Coy.

15440 Cpl. W.P. Steel, 8th York and Lancs.,
formerly 15440 Pte. "B" Coy.

34853 L.-Cpl. J.L. Wilson, 8th York and Lancs.,
formerly 15813 Pte. "D" Coy.

†15583 Pte. R.D. Frame, 2nd H.L.I.,
formerly Pte. "C" Coy.

15389 Cpl. D. Murray, 16th H.L.I.,
formerly L.-Cpl. "B" Coy.

15373 Sergt. F.J. M'Clusky, 2nd H.L.I.,
formerly L.-Cpl., "A" Coy.

—— Sergt. A. M'auslan, R.E.,
formerly 15365 L.-Cpl. "A" Coy.

16192 L.-Cpl. H. M'Killop, 16th H.L.I.,
formerly L.-Cpl. "A" Coy.

Every effort has been made by reference to the Battalion Records, by advertising and otherwise, to make these lists complete. The (original) editors will much regret should there be unfortunately any omissions.

List of officers who were granted commissions in the Battalion on its formation and posted to companies as shewn.

Lieut.-Colonel D.S. Morton, V.D.

"A" Company.
> Major W.J. Paul
> (Commanding).
> Captain W.W. Morton.
> Lieut. R.T. Neilson.
> Lieut. J.B. Macbrayne.
> Lieut. Gardner.
> Lieut. G.R.S. Paterson.

"B" Company.
> Major J.R. Young

---

†Since deceased.

130

(Commanding).
Captain J. Russell.
Lieut. G.V.M. Boyd.
Lieut. A.J. Begg.
2nd Lieut. R. Scott.

"C" Company.
Major W. Auld, V.D.
(Commanding).
Captain W.H. Anderson.
Lieut. A.J. Ferguson.
Lieut. F.D. Morton.
Lieut. A.S. Millar.
Lieut. J.S. Sharp.

"D" Company.
Captain E. Hutchison
(Commanding).
Captain J. MCM. Mitchell.
2nd Lieut. P.G. Symington.
Lieut. R.W. Cassell.
2nd Lieut. D. Kitchen.
Lieut. J.M. Brown.

Lieut. and Quartermaster A.E. Slade.

Lieut. D.R. Kirkpatrick, R.A.M.C. (attached).

The Battalion was successively under the command of:—

Colonel D.S. Morton, C.M.G., V.D.

Lieut.-Colonel W.J. Paul.

Lieut.-Colonel F.R.F. Sworder,
Gordon Highlanders.

Lieut.-Colonel J. Inglis, C.M.G., D.S.O.,
Highland Light Infantry.

THE FOLLOWING "OTHER RANKS" OF THE BATTALION WERE
GRANTED COMMISSIONS IN THE BATTALION.

2nd Lt. W.M. Alexander,	Killed in Action,	01/07/16
2nd Lt. J.R. Beckett,	Wounded in Action,	01/07/16
	Died of Wounds,	04/07/16
2nd Lt. J.L. Brodie, M.C.,	To 15th H.L.I, on disbandment.	
★2nd Lt. J.M. Brown.	—	—

2nd Lt. J.N. Carpenter, M.C.,	Killed in Action,	01/07/16
2nd Lt. J. Chapman,	Wounded in Action,	01/07/16
*2nd Lt. H.C. Colvil.	—	—
2nd Lt. P.N. Cunningham,	Killed in Action,	02/12/17
Captain E. Dobson,	Killed in Action,	10/07/17
Captain A.N. Drysdale, M.C.,	Died of Wounds,	15/04/17
Lieut. A.S. Elsworth,	Wounded in Action,	01/07/16
	Wounded in Action,	--/08/17
*2nd Lt. J.W. Fraser.	—	—
*2nd Lt. P.H. Graham.	—	—
2nd Lt. G.G. Henderson,	Killed in Action,	06/08/16
*2nd Lt. H.G. Hendry.	—	—
2nd Lt. W.A. Herron,	Wounded in Action,	--/08/17
Lieut. Jas. Kelly, D.C.M.,	—	—
2nd Lt. A.D. Laird,	Killed in Action,	01/07/16
Captain T.P. Locking,	—	—
Captain J.F. Morrison,	Killed in Action,	18/11/16
Captain J.S. Marr,	Killed in Action,	18/11/16
Captain H. M'Robert,	To General Staff (Staff Captain).	
Captain J.L. M'Connell, M.C.,	To General List (Staff Captain).	
2nd Lt. J.M. Macarthur,	To T.M. Battery	
Captain A.G. Marshall,	Killed in Action,	12/02/17
*2nd Lt. H.R. Orr.	—	—
2nd Lt. J. Osborne,	Killed in Action,	02/12/17
2nd Lt. H.R. Peat,	Wounded in Action,	10/07/17
*2nd Lt. F.H. Pooley.	—	—
*2nd Lt. F.A. Russell.	—	—
2nd Lt. J.C. Todd,	Killed in Action,	27/06/17
*2nd Lt. G.B. Walker.	—	—
2nd Lt. C.S. Williamson,	Wounded in Action,	--/08/17
2nd Lt. D.G. Younger,	Killed in Action,	1/07/16

* These officers did not serve with the Battalion in France. The ranks noted are those which they held previous to Embarkation.

ROLL OF WARRANT OFFICERS, NON-COMMISSIONED OFFICERS AND MEN, WHO JOINED THE CHAMBER OF COMMERCE BATTALION FROM 12TH SEPTEMBER, 1914, TILL EMBARKATION OF BATTALION, 22ND NOVEMBER, 1915.

All the undernoted joined the Battalion as Privates. The Ranks shown are those attained previous to Embarkation.

Reg. No. Rank. Name.

15200 L.-Corpl. Donald, Alex. Watt.
15201 Pte. Buchanan, Joseph Robt.
15202 Pte. Pert, David.
15203 Pte. Love, Alan.
15204 Sergt. Todd, Matthew G.
15205 R.S.M. Kelly, J.
15206 R.Q.M.S. Keith, T.
15207 O.R./Q.M.S. Copland, J.
15208 Pte. Anderson, Wm.
15209 C.Q.M.S. Ferguson, A. W.
15210 C.S.M. M'Clusky, F.
15211 C.Q.M.S. Williams, E.A.
15212 C.S.M. Garrow, J.C.
15213 C.Q.M.S. Ferris, H.
15214 C.S.M. Dunsmore, W.
15215 C.Q.M.S. Core, T.M.
15216 C.S.M. Taylor, G.H.
15217 Pte. Seaton, James.
15218 Pte. Adam, Arthur Wm.
15219 Pte. Armstrong, John.
15220 Pte. Allan, Peter.
15221 Pte. Arthur, David.
15222 Pte. Anderson, Matthew.
15223 Pte. Anderson, Wm.
15224 Pte. Aitkenhead, R.T.
15225 Pte. Adam, Andrew Rolland.
15226 Pte. Angus, L.S.
15227 Pte. Allan, John.
15228 Pte. Allan, Wm. Taylor.
15229 Pte. Andrew, Wm.
15230 Pte. Blair, David A.
15231 Pte. Binnie, Jas. W.

15232 Pte. Brown, James.
15233 L.-Sergt. Baxter, Alex. C.
15234 Pte. Bates, John R.
15235 Pte. Brown, Alex.
15236 Pte. Barr, Rich.
15237 Pte. Brown, T.J.
15238 Pte. Booth, Charles.
15239 Pte. Binnie, David W.
15240 Pte. Barr, F.C.G.
15241 Pte. Burgess, James.
15242 Pte. Baxter, Wm.
15243 Pte. Campbell, B. M'C.
15244 Pte. Clark, J.N.P.
15245 Pte. Calder, Alex.
15246 Sergt. Cochrane, J.C.
15247 Pte. Clark, James.
15248 Pte. Cox, C.Wm.
15249 Pte. Craig, R.B.
15250 Pte. Campbell, E.
15251 L.-Cpl. Cuthbert, Arthur.
15252 Pte. Cunninghame, Douglas.
15253 L.-Cpl. Coogan, Malcolm.
15254 Pte. Cuthbert, J.C.
15255 L.-Cpl. Chapman, John.
15256 Pte. Crombie, James.
15257 Pte. Caw, Wm.
15258 Pte. Collins, A.E.
15259 Sergt. Carnan, John.
15260 Pte. Currie, Neil T.
15261 Pte. Clark, Geo.
15262 Cpl. Drever, Wm.
15263 Cpl. Dobbie, Robt. Wm.
15264 L.-Sergt. Douglas, John.
15265 Pte. Donnelly, Wm. John.
15266 Pte. Deans, Geo. W.
15267 L.-Cpl. Dickson, Thomas P.
15268 Pte. Dow, Samuel Hugh.
15269 L.-Cpl. Dymock, H.M.
15270 Pte. Dunlop, Robt.
15271 Pte. White, T.W.D.

15272 Pte. Davidson, Thomas Y.
15273 L.-Cpl. Drysdale, Alex. O.
15274 Sergt. Drummond, Mark.
15275 Pte. Dingwall, R. M'F.
15276 Pte. Duncan, Robert G.
15277 Cpl. Fleming, John.
15278 Pte. Forrest, E.
15279 Pte. Findlay, David.
15280 Pte. Fortune, George R.
15281 Pte. Finlinson, Arthur B.
15282 A/C.Q.M.S. Ferguson, Alex.
15283 Pte. Frew, James Allen.
15284 Pte. Fraser, Alex.
15285 Pte. Fraser, Donald.
15286 L.-Sergt. Gowans, James.
15287 L.-Cpl. Grigsby, A.H.
15288 Pte. Gillespie, A.A.
15289 L.-Cpl. Gannaway, George Edward.
15290 Pte. Grigg, Stanley J.
15291 L.-Cpl. Gill, John.
15292 Pte. Goodall, Robert L.
15293 Pte. Gemmel, Alex.
15294 L.-Cpl. Glassford, Alex. S.
15295 L.-Cpl. Griffiths, J.L.
15296 Pte. Galloway, Charles.
15297 Pte. Gardiner, William.
15298 Pte. Gray, Alex.
15299 Pte. Gudgeon, Thomas W.
15300 Pte. Gibbon, Edward.
15301 Pte. Graham, William R.
15302 Pte. Gowans, Alex.
15303 L.-Cpl. Haddow, Robert B.
15304 Pte. Hovell, Alex.
15305 Pte. Haddon, R. M'K.
15306 Pte. Henderson, Robert.
15307 Pte. Highet, Andrew.
15308 Pte. Horsley, B.T.
15309 Pte. Herbert, Peter C.
15310 L.-Cpl. Hirst, George.
15311 Pte. Hay, Neil T.

15312 Pte. Hyslop, William.
15313 Pte. Hubbard, William.
15314 Pte. Hutchison, William Ramsay.
15315 L.-Cpl. Hutton, David.
15316 Pte. Hagen, John.
15317 Pte. Hunter, John Wilson.
15318 Pte. Hay, John.
15319 Sergt. Hamilton, John.
15320 Pte. Hardie, Gordon D.
15321 Pte. Herbert, Morris.
15322 Pte. Hemphill, Archibald.
15323 Pte. Johnston, Samuel.
15324 Pte. Johnstone, Robert M.
15325 L.-Cpl. Jackson, David.
15326 Pte. Jarvie, William Robert.
15327 Pte. Jackson, John A.
15328 Pte. Johnstone, Kenneth.
15329 Pte. Inglis, John.
15330 Pte. Kelly, Thomas.
15331 Pte. Liddell, George.
15332 Pte. Livingstone, James H.
15333 Pte. Lochhead, Robert Allan.
15334 Pte. Lorimer, John William.
15335 Pte. Livingston, Alex. Bryson.
15336 Pte. Love, Robert.
15337 Pte. Lyons, John M.
15338 Pte. Morrison, James F.
15339 Pte. Morrison, James Smith.
15340 Pte. Miller, John.
15341 Pte. Milne, William.
15342 L.-Cpl. Murdoch, William.
15343 Pte. Munro, Hector.
15344 Pte. Muir, D.L.
15345 Pte. Muir, Robert E.R.
15346 L.-Cpl. M'Callum, Colin.
15347 Pte. M'Aulay, Archibald.
15348 L.-Sergt. M'Naught, James.
15349 Pte. M'Millan, Daniel.
15350 Pte. M'Kendrick, Alex.
15351 Sergt. M'Letchie, John B.

15352 Pte. M'Leod, Alex. G.
15353 Pte. M'Murtrie, Dougald M'K.
15354 L.-Cpl. M'Gregor, James R.
15355 Pte. Macdonald, John Grant.
15356 Pte. M'Neil, Joseph.
15357 Pte. McLauchlan, John H.
15358 Pte. MacDougall, Duncan.
15359 Pte. M'Taggart, Duncan.
15360 Pte. M'Crone, Robert.
15361 Pte. MacAllan, Thomas Alex.
15362 Pte. M'Farlane, James.
15363 Pte. M'Nair, Allan Gilmour.
15364 Pte. M'Lean, Hugh.
15365 L.-Cpl. M'Auslan, Alex.
15366 Pte. M'Dougall, Peter.
15367 Sergt. M'Taggart, William Kerr.
15368 Pte. M'Neill, James.
15369 Pte. M'Lachlan, Louis Alex.
15370 Pte. M'Hugh, Matthew.
15371 Pte. M'Vake, Robert.
15372 Pte. M'Garrity, Michael.
15373 L.-Cpl. M'Clusky, F. John.
15374 Pte. M'Phail, John.
15375 Sergt. M'Arthur, John M'L.
15376 Pte. M'Naught, Duncan.
15377 Pte. M'Neil, Charles M'G.
15378 Pte. M'Corquodale, Archibald.
15379 Pte. M'Meechan, David Cowan.
15380 Cpl. M'Williams, J.
15381 Pte. M'Culloch, George Neil.
15382 Sergt. M'Gibbon, William.
15383 Pte. Munro, Alex. M'L.
15384 Pte. Miller, David.
15385 Pte. Munro, John.
15386 Pte. Morrison, Donald.
15387 L.-Cpl. Marshall, Allan Gow.
15388 Pte. Mailer, Andrew.
15389 Pte. Murray, David.
15390 Pte. Mowat, John Watt.
15391 Pte. Morrison, Andrew.

15392 Pte. Miller, James.
15393 Pte. Maitland, William.
15394 Pte. Millar, Angus.
15395 Cpl. Miller, James.
15396 L.-Cpl. Martin, David.
15397 Pte. Morrison, Robert.
15398 Pte. May, William Walker.
15399 L.-Cpl. Maxwell, Claude.
15400 Pte. Meek, George.
15401 Pte. Muir, James.
15402 Pte. Milner, Thomas.
15403 L.-Sergt. Milne, James Wallace.
15404 Sergt. May, C.S.
15405 Pte. Menzies, Peter D.
15406 Pte. Orr, John Leslie.
15407 Pte. Pinkerton, Gavin.
15408 Pte. Paterson, Robert.
15409 Pte. Philp, Robert C.P.
15410 Pte. Paterson, John.
15411 Pte. Pattison, Robert M'P.
15412 Pte. Phillips, Alexander R.H.
15413 Pte. Preston, William Parker.
15414 L.-Cpl. Palmer, C.L.
15415 Sergt. Ritchie, Thomas.
15416 L.-Cpl. Robertson, George Tennant.
15417 Pte. Ritchie, William.
15418 Sergt. Robertson, John S.
15419 L.-Cpl. Reid, Donald M.
15420 Pte. Russell, William.
15421 Pte. Roy, George Allan.
15422 Pte. Ritchie, Robert F.
15423 Pte. Rogers, David Anderson.
15424 Pte. Russell, Samuel.
15425 L.-Cpl. Rait, Patrick W.
15426 Pte. Spence, Telford.
15427 Pte. Slater, Albert Ernest.
15428 Pte. Stuart, Charles M'D.
15429 Pte. Scott, William James.
15430 Pte. Somerville, James.
15431 Pte. Struthers, Hugh E.

15432 Pte. Scott, George K.
15433 Pte. Stark, David.
15434 Pte. Sutherland, Thomas N.
15435 Pte. Scott, Joe.
15436 Pte. Strachan, Andrew R.
15437 Cpl. Scott, Archibald.
15438 Pte. Stokes, Arthur C.
15439 Pte. Swan, Allan.
15440 Pte. Steel, W.P.
15441 Pte. Stewart, John C.
15442 Cpl. Stevenson, John.
15443 Pte. Scott, William.
15444 Pte. Simpson, Walter.
15445 Pte. Scott, William P.
15446 Pte. Scott, Robert Neil.
15447 Pte. Samuels, James M.
15448 Pte. Small, Samuel.
15449 Sergt. Sanders, Sydney T.
15450 Pte. Thomson, John Hill.
15451 Pte. Torrance, E.
15452 Cpl. Timpson, Charles.
15453 Pte. Thomson, James.
15454 Pte. Thomson, David M.
15455 Sergt. Thomson, H.W.H.
15456 Sergt. Thomson, William James.
15457 Pte. Turnbull, George King.
15458 Sergt. Taylor, Herbert G.
15459 Pte. Thom, Matthew F.
15460 L.-Sergt. Taylor, David Alex.
15461 Pte. Wark, James Allen.
15462 Pte. Wallace, John.
15463 Pte. Warnock, James.
15464 Sergt. Watts, Frank M.W.
15465 Sergt. Woyka, Alex. G.
15466 Cpl. Wyman, Sydney.
15467 Sergt. Wishart, Alfred.
15468 Pte. Bruce, Thomas.
15469 Pte. Webster, James.
15470 Sergt. Watson, John.
15471 Pte. Waterman, R.

15472 Pte. Willock, Thos. B.
15473 Pte. Wallace, Robert Kerr.
15474 Pte. Young, William.
15475 Pte. Young, Robert.
15476 Pte. Finlayson, William Thomson.
15477 Pte. Atkinson, William.
15478 Pte. Alexander, W.M.
15479 Pte. Alexander, Walter.
15480 Pte. Angus, Thomas C.
15481 Cpl. Abercromby, Archibald Alex.
15482 Pte. Alston, James.
15483 Pte. Arbuckle, Alex.
15484 Pte. M'Arthur, Alex.
15485 Sergt. Angus, William Clark.
15486 Pte. Atkins, William J.L.
15487 L.-Cpl. Allan, James.
15488 Pte. Andrews, Matthew M'Kay.
15489 Pte. Biggs, Frank A.
15490 Pte. Bennett, James S.
15491 Pte. Crawford, Matthew.
15492 L.-Cpl. Black, Alex.
15493 Pte. Barron, John F.
15494 Pte. Broadhead, John R.
15495 Pte. Baxter, David John.
15496 Pte. Ballantyne, Francis.
15497 Pte. Burleigh, John.
15498 Pte. Bryce, Thomas.
15499 Pte. Barkley, Martin Bell.
15500 Pte. Barclay, John.
15501 Pte. Barton, Alex. Baird.
15502 Pte. Broadhead, Alex. G.
15503 Pte. Bailley, William N.
15504 Pte. Brown, John M'D.
15505 Pte. Barton, Robert L.
15506 Pte. Borthwick, H.H.
15507 A/C.S.M. Reith, Stephen D.
15508 Pte. Bebbington, John Vernon.
15509 Pte. Baird, H. Thompson.
15510 Pte. Bruce, John Charles.
15511 Pte. Provan, George.

15512 Pte. Brooke, Robert L.
15513 Pte. Buchanan, Robert W.H.
15514 Pte. Buchanan, William.
15515 Pte. Bailley, A.R.
15516 A/C.S.M. Ballantyne, William N.
15517 Sergt. Brown, William P.
15518 Cpl. Brown, Robert S.
15519 Pte. Cameron, Alexander.
15520 Sergt. Drummond, William.
15521 Pte. Drysdale, Alex. N.
15522 Pte. Dobson, Edward.
15523 L.-Sergt. Dunlop, James.
15524 L.-Cpl. Carswell, John C.
15525 Pte. Duncan, Thomas.
15526 Pte. Crockett, George P.
15527 L.-Cpl. Callan, John.
15528 Pte. Cameron, Malcolm C.
15529 Pte. Cooper, William.
15530 Pte. Craig, James M.
15531 Pte. Cowan, John.
15532 Pte. Carpenter, John M.
15533 Pte. Curie, Robert.
15534 Pte. Chalmers, Thomas M.
15535 L.-Sergt. Cook, Thomas.
15536 Sig.-Cpl. Craig, Thomas.
15537 Pte. Fleming, Harry C.
15538 Pte. M'Intyre, D.C.
15539 Pte. Crombie, Robt. A.
15540 Pte. Campbell, Thomas C.
15541 Pte. Cross, Archibald David.
15542 Pte. Cruickshank, Alex. A.
15543 Pte. Channing, H.H.
15544 L.-Cpl. Cullen, Matthew.
15545 Pte. Campbell, William T.
15546 Pte. Christison, Robert Colin.
15547 Cpl. Crocker, John.
15548 Pte. Cameron, Alex. C.
15549 Pte. Cumming, A. Smith.
15550 L.-Sergt. Cuthbertson, Charles S.
15551 Pte. Craig, Thomas.

15552 L.-Cpl. Craig, A.B.
15553 Pte. Craig, John.
15554 L.-Cpl. Crawford, Thomas.
15555 L.-Cpl. Corbett, William S.
15556 Pte. Crinean, Charles.
15557 Pte. Carmichael, James A.
15558 Cpl. Davidson, Albert.
15559 Cpl. Davidson, John.
15560 Pte. Dawes, Harry E.
15561 L.-Cpl. Davie, Harry Craig.
15562 Pte. Dunsmuir, A.G.
15563 Pte. Dow, William John.
15564 Pte. Dixon, Charles.
15565 Pte. Dott, Robert Wilson.
15566 Cpl. Erskine, Ralph.
15567 Pte. Elliot, James Kirk.
15568 Pte. Elsworth, A.S.
15569 Sergt. Ellery, Albert Charles.
15570 Pte. Eggert, Walter.
15571 Pte. Edmond, George G.
15572 Pte. Fisher, Thomas C.
15573 Pte. Fleming, John J.
15574 L.-Sergt. Fraser, Samuel.
15575 Pte. Fergus, Robert B.
15576 Pte. Forrest, Archibald.
15577 Pte. Frame, William D.
15578 Pte. Foulger, Horace William.
15579 Pte. Freeman, Michael.
15580 Pte. Fraser, James W.
15581 Pte. Fraser, Campbell N.
15582 Pte. Follett, Arthur V.
15583 Pte. Frame, Robert D.
15584 Pte. Ferguson, Hume.
15585 Pte. Freeland, Thomas S.
15586 Pte. Fleming, Allan.
15587 Pte. Falconer, J. Alex.
15588 L.-Sergt. Fullerton, William L.
15589 Pte. Flintoff, R. Alex.
15590 Pte. Ford, William Graham.
15591 Pte. Fraser, William Alex.

15592 Pte. Finlayson, James.
15593 Pte. Garrioch, Alex.
15594 L.-Cpl. Gray, Donald.
15595 Pte. Galloway, John H.
15596 L.-Cpl. Greig, Gilbert.
15597 Pte. Guthrie, Robert Yates.
15598 Pte. Gauld, Ernest G.
15599 Pte. Graham, Patrick H.
15600 Pte. Graham, William.
15601 Pte. Garrioch, J. M'K.
15602 Pte. Graham, George.
15603 Pte. Gilfillan, William.
15604 Pte. Galt, Adam.
15605 Pte. Gibson, Allan D.
15606 L.-Cpl. Deans, A. Gibson.
15607 Pte. Grandison, Arthur A.
15608 Pte. Gemmell, A.S.
15610 Pte. Gray, Robert Love.
15611 Pte. Hamilton, James.
15612 Pte. Hutchison, George M'F.
15613 Pte. Hall, David S.
15614 Pte. Henderson, George G.
15615 L.-Cpl. Hamilton, William.
15616 Pte. Hamilton, Samuel.
15617 Pte. Hamilton, William John.
15618 Pte. Henderson, James.
15619 Pte. Hutton, John Graham.
15620 Pte. Haddow, John Haig.
15621 L.-Cpl. Hunter, James Crawford.
15622 Pte. Harper, John M.
15623 Pte. Herron, William A.
15624 Pte. Horne, Walter D.
15625 Pte. Hamilton, William.
15626 Sergt. Haft, Julian.
15627 Pte. Houstoun, Alexander G.
15628 L.-Cpl. Harvie, Alex. W.
15629 Cpl. Hogg, William.
15630 Pte. Hutchison, James M.
15631 Pte. Hutcheson, Thomas.
15632 Pte. Howie, Kenneth M.

15633 L.-Cpl. Hamilton, J.F.
15634 Cpl. Henderson, Robert.
15635 Pte. Howie, John Love.
15636 Pte. Haggerty, Thomas.
15637 Pte. Imrie, Frank M.
15638 Pte. Irvine, Alex. Garven.
15639 Pte. Inrig, Alex. George.
15640 Pte. Jenkins, John B.
15641 Pte. Kean, James M'Lean.
15642 Pte. Kinloch, Peter S.
15643 Pte. Kerr, Andrew A.
15644 Pte. Kinghorn, Arthur A.A.
15645 Pte. Kennedy, James.
15646 L.-Cpl. Keast, Norman R.
15647 Pte. Knight, Alex.
15648 Cpl. Kedslie, John Kay.
15649 Sergt. Kennedy, David.
15650 L.-Cpl. Lothian, William.
15651 L.-Cpl. Leask, Andrew D.
15652 Pte. Munro, Thomas A.
15653 Cpl. Miller, Alex. L.
15654 Pte. Marr, James Scott.
15655 Cpl. Lindsay, Douglas A.B.
15656 Pte. Love, David A.
15657 Sergt. Locking, Thomas P.
15658 Pte. Lucas, Charles Walker.
15659 Pte. Leckie, Robert G.
15660 Pte. Laird, Arthur D.
15661 Pte. Linn, William Gemmell.
15662 L.-Cpl. Leishman, Thomas.
15663 Pte. Livie, John Fletcher.
15664 Sergt. Lang, Archibald.
15665 Pte. Lindsay, John Caird.
15666 Pte. Love, Alex. James.
15667 Pte. Lawson, H. Gibson.
15668 Pte. Levy, Barnet.
15669 Pte. Locke, Norman.
15670 L.-Cpl. Lees, Charles.
15671 L.-Cpl. Moses, James.
15672 Pte. Miller, Davie.

15673 Pte. Maitland, Alex. M'Lean.
15674 L.-Cpl. More, James.
15675 Pte. Miller, George.
15676 Sergt. Marshall, John.
15677 Sergt. Maxwell, Joseph.
15678 Pte. Murray, Charles De B.
15679 Pte. Murray, Archibald William.
15680 Pte. Miller, Archibald A.
15681 Pte. Murdoch, Robert.
15682 L.-Cpl. Mackin, Stephen James.
15683 Pte. Moir, Alex. Hamilton.
15684 Pte. Morton, John T.K.
15685 L.-Sergt. Miller, James Alex.
15686 Cpl. Murray, Thomas H.
15687 L.-Cpl. Murdoch, Archibald.
15688 Pte. Miller, Arthur T.
15689 Pte. Melville, David W.
15690 Pte. Mills, Duncan B.
15691 Pte. Mills, David M'A.
15692 Sergt. Morrison, Thomas E.
15693 Pte. Morton, Thomas I.
15694 Pte. Miller, John.
15695 Pte. Miller, Alex. Hume.
15696 Pte. M'Naughton, Callum Arthur.
15697 Pte. M'Millan, William A.
15698 L.-Cpl. M'Gibbon, John.
15699 Pte. M'Feat, Fred.
15700 Pte. M'Aviney, James.
15701 Pte. M'Lelland, George H.
15702 Sig.-Sergt. M'Intosh, John R.
15703 Pte. M'Gavin, Colin M'K.
15704 Pte. MacMillan, Donald D.
15705 Pte. M'Crae, James.
15706 Pte. MacMillan, John.
15707 Pte. Macdonald, James.
15708 L.-Cpl. MacDougall, Charles S.
15709 Pte. M'Connell, John L.
15710 Pte. MacDougall, John A.
15711 Pte. M'Donald, Duncan.
15712 Sergt. MacMillan, Alex.

15713 Cpl. M'Culloch, W.
15714 Pte. M'Auley, Robert.
15715 Pte. M'Nicol, James F.
15716 Pte. M'Leod, Donald M'K.
15717 Cpl. M'Arthur, Neil M'C.
15718 Pte. M'Gee, Gilmour Brown.
15719 Pte. M'Arthur, Hugh.
15720 Pte. M'Intosh, Donald.
15721 Pte. Clark, Robert O.
15722 Sergt. M'Andrew, William.
15723 Pte. Provan, George Weir.
15724 L.-Sergt. M'Kenzie, E.P.
15725 Pte. Bull, Harold.
15726 L.-Cpl. Scott, W.P.
15727 Pte. Grandison, William A.
15728 Pte. M'Lintock, Hugh C.
15729 Pte. Baird, John.
15730 L.-Cpl. Young, John R.
15731 Pte. Adamson, Thomas N.
15732 Pte. Dawson, John.
15733 Pte. M'Dougall, Alan.
15734 L.-Cpl. Norris, James H.
15735 Pte. Neilson, William George.
15736 Pte. Orr, Harry Ross.
15737 Pte. Purdie, John D.
15738 Pte. Paterson, G.K.
15739 Pte. Pollock, William G.
15740 Pte. Pearson, William L.
15741 Pte. Younger, David G.
15742 L.-Cpl. M'Rae, Donald.
15743 Pte. MacGregor, William D.
15744 Pte. Watson, William O.
15745 Pte. Wilson, Allan Jackson.
15746 Pte. Macpherson, Angus.
15747 Pte. Mackinley, Alex. W.
15748 Sergt. MacGregor, Fred. M.
15749 Pte. M'Robbie, David H.
15750 Pte. M'Houll, K.
15751 Pte. M'Phail, Thomas W.
15752 L.-Cpl. M'Intyre, James.

15753 L.-Cpl. M'Gavin, N.P.
15754 Pte. Paul, Robert M'L.
15755 L.-Cpl. Pyper, Henry James.
15756 L.-Cpl. Pickering, Robert Y.
15757 Pte. Paterson, Robert.
15758 Pte. Paterson, George M.
15759 Pte. Purdie, William.
15760 Pte. Robertson, William B.
15761 Pte. Russell, H. M'P.
15762 Pte. Rogerson, James Muir.
15763 Pte. Rudd, David H.
15764 Pte. Riley, Thomas D.
15765 Pte. Rogerson, John Elliot.
15766 Pte. Robertson, William Telfer.
15767 Pte. M'Rorie, Robert.
15768 L.-Cpl. Rolland, Charles D.
15769 Cpl. Russell, Fred. Alex.
15770 Pte. Rose, John Alex.
15771 Pte. Ross, James.
15772 L.-Cpl. Robertson, Robert Speirs.
15773 Pte. Rankin, Colin.
15774 Pte. Roper, William H.
15775 Cpl. Roberts, John.
15776 Pte. Robertson, David.
15777 Pte. Roxburgh, Thomas L.[116]
15778 Pte. Muir, Norman R.
15779 Pte. Ritchie, Edgar.
15780 Pte. Ritchie, William Stewart.
15781 Pte. Reid, William Hamilton.
15782 Pte. Spence, Donald W.
15783 A/C.S.M. Sturton, James.
15784 Pte. Smith, William Edward.
15785 Sergt. West, John.
15786 Cpl. Shannon, Andrew A.
15787 Pte. Stark, Robert L.
15788 Pte. Smellie, John.
15789 Pte. Sprott, Samuel.
15790 Pte. Stark, James T.
15791 Pte. Steel, David F.
15792 Pte. Sterling, John L.

15793 Pte. Scouler, James Tott.
15794 Pte. Sloan, Allan T.
15795 Pte. Stewart, George R.
15796 Pte. Stevenson, William.
15797 Pte. Scott, Robert Spence.
15798 Cpl. Stirling, Archibald B.
15799 Pte. Stroud, E.H.N.
15800 L.-Cpl. Smillie, James M'G.
15801 Pte. Scott, Walter.
15802 Pte. Stewart, Duncan H.
15803 Pte. Taggart, Henry R.
15804 Pte. Tough, Thomas S.
15805 L.-Sergt. Thomson, James C.
15806 Cpl. Terrie, Andrew Black.
15807 Pte. Turnbull, Thomas.
15808 Pte. Wood, Duncan B.
15809 Pte. Warren, A.B.
15810 Pte. Wurr, Herbert Joseph.
15811 Pte. Walker, Norman M.L.
15812 Pte. Wright, William B.
15813 Pte. Wilson, James L.
15814 Pte. Walker, Alexander.
15815 Pte. White, John B.
15816 Pte. Walker, Ernest G.
15817 Pte. White, George.
15818 Pte. Watson, Robert M'L.
15819 L.-Sergt. Wingate, James L.
15820 Pte. Welsh, Thomas Morrison.
15821 Pte. Wilson, A.K.
15822 Pte. Westwater, Donald U.
15823 Pte. Wilson, Henry.
15824 Pte. Watson, William N.
15825 Pte. Walker, George B.
15826 Pte. Wilson, Robert C.
15827 L.-Cpl. Waugh, Thomas.
15828 Pte. Young, James B.
15829 Pte. Young, John.
15830 Pte. Yuill, L.
15831 Pte. Young, Alex.
15832 L.-Sergt. Anderson, Robert.

15833 Pte. Allan, James.
15834 Pte. Barbour, John.
15835 Pte. Bowman, Joseph W.
15836 Pte. Brown, J. Lindsay.
15837 Pte. Baird, James.
15838 Pte. Beckett, James R.
15839 L.-Cpl. Brownlie, James M'H.
15840 Pte. Carson, F.R.
15841 Sergt. Cohen, Arthur M.
15842 Pte. Cowley, Victor.
15843 Sergt. Cowden, Alex.
15844 Pte. Dixon, Wilfrid.
15845 C.S.M. Dobbie, William.
15846 Pte. Finlay, John.
15847 Pte. Forrest, George.
15848 Pte. Fulton, C.S.
15849 Trans. Sergt. Fraser, Walter.
15850 Pte. Graham, Alex. H.
15851 Pte. Grant, Kenneth.
15852 Pte. Gibb, Thomas.
15853 Pte. Grassick, Charles A.
15854 Pte. Haddow, Hugh P.
15855 Pte. Hill, Sydney Thomas.
15856 Pte. Holmes, James.
15857 Cpl. Houston, William.
15858 Pte. Inglis, Robert.
15859 Pte. Jones, G. Philip.
15860 Pte. Leask, Ralph.
15861 Pte. Leckie, Andrew.
15862 Pte. Learmond, Victor.
15863 Pte. Mackie, Robert Neil.
15864 L.-Cpl. MacKay, John.
15865 Pte. MacRobert, Harry.
15866 Sergt. Mather, W.
15867 Pte. Moreland, Joseph.
15868 Pte. Millar, James.
15869 Pte. Morton, James G.
15870 Pte. M'Kenzie, M.A.
15871 Pte. M'Kee, Robert.
15872 Pte. M'Kelvie, Andrew.

15873 Pte. M'Kinnon, Donald.
15874 Pte. Palmer, Ernest.
15875 Sergt. Paterson, Duncan.
15876 L.-Cpl. Pyper, James F.
15877 Pte. Reid, David.
15878 Pte. Rhind, Andrew.
15879 Pte. Richardson, James W.
15880 Pte. Ritchie, John Allan.
15881 Pte. Robertson, James.
15882 Pte. Russell, George C.
15883 Pte. Rutherford, Edward P.
15884 Cpl. Cameron, David D.
15885 Pte. Stewart, William.
15886 T./Sergt. Summers, Alan Y.
15887 Pte. Thomson, Robert.
15888 Sergt. Turnbull, J. Y.
15889 Pte. Watson, Alex.
15890 Pte. Watson, Peter S.
15891 Pte. Wood, John Hamilton.
15892 Pte. Wilson, Robert B.
15893 Pte. Ramage, Peter.
15894 Pte. Stevens, Montague.
15895 Pte. Mossman, William.
15896 L.-Cpl. Wright, Colin S.
15897 Pte. Harvey, Edward A.
15898 Pte. Kirkpatrick, Arthur J.
15899 Pte. Kie, George.
15900 Pte. Walker, Thomas.
15901 Cpl. Mann, R.G.
15902 Pte. Meldrum, George.
15903 Pte. Hunter, Matthew C.
15904 Sergt. Abercrombie, H. M'P.
15905 Pte. Kelly, James.
15906 Pte. Waugh, Robert.
15907 Pte. Pettigrew, William.
15908 Pte. Connell, Archibald.
15909 S./Sergt. Duffus, Hugh W.
15910 Pte. Baines, Donald.
15911 L.-Cpl. Coltart, John S.
15912 Pte. Hutchison, James.

15913 Pte. Annand, James S.
15914 L.-Cpl. M'Kenzie, Hugh F.
15915 Pte. Guthrie, William.
15916 Cpl. Steven, Alex.
15917 Pte. Hoole, Roland Allan.
15918 Pte. Duff, Robert.
15919 Pte. M'Lean, Alex.
15920 Pte. Paterson, J.
15921 Pte. Maxwell, Herbert S.
15922 Pte. Simpson, A.D.H.
15923 Pte. MacFarlane, N.
15924 Pte. Casey, George H.
15925 Pte. Baillies, Oswald.
15926 Pte. Nowery, Alex. F.
15927 L.-Cpl. Thomson, Alex. D.
15928 Cpl. Brackenridge, John.
15929 Pte. Hutchison, Alfred.
15930 L.-Cpl. Kunzle, Paul.
15931 L.-Cpl. Nisbet, John D.
15932 Pte. Taylor, Thomas T.
15933 Pte. Long, Cunningham.
15934 Pte. Wark, John.
15935 L.-Cpl. Kerr, Robert.
15936 Pte. Aitken, Wilfred.
15937 Cpl. Farnell, Fred.
15938 Sergt. Watson, Alex. G.
15939 Pte. M'Lean, A.
15940 L.-Cpl. Yuill, Andrew.
15941 Pte. M'Culloch, Charles M.
15942 A/C.S.M. Lochhead, Alex. W.
15943 Pte. Glen, James.
15944 Pte. Yates, Norman.
15945 Cpl. McNaught, John.
15946 Pte. Whyte, Duncan.
15947 L.-Cpl. Robertson, John.
15948 Sergt. M'Call, William.
15949 Pte. Vallance, Harold L.
15950 Pte. Gray, James.
15951 Sergt. Howard, John B.S.
15952 Pte. Anderson, John William.

15953 Pte. Brodie, Alex.
15954 Sergt. Headrick, William Smith.
15955 A/C.S.M. Tilley, Richard.
15956 Sergt. Stewart, William S.
15957 Sergt. Parker, James R.
15958 Pte. Maconochie, William K.
15959 Sergt. Ritchie, William F.
15960 Pte. Kyle, John.
15961 L.-Sergt. Hughes, Arthur.
15962 Pte. Farish, Samuel.
15963 Pte. Ritchie, Robert.
15964 L.-Sergt. Osborne, John.
15965 Pte. Kerr, John.
15966 Pte. Gemmell, Norman L.
15967 Pte. Grant, Alex. A.
15968 Pte. Inglis, John James.
15969 L.-Cpl. Turner, Elliot D.
15970 L.-Cpl. Cunningham, Peter N.
15971 Pte. Gilchrist, Thomas A.
15972 Sergt. Wilson, A.P.
15973 L.-Cpl. Dickson, William.
15974 Pte. Orchardson, Archibald.
15975 L.-Cpl. Watson, Andrew.
15976 Pte. Thorburn, James.
15977 Pte. Sharp, Alex. Thomas.
15978 Pte. Hastings, Edward H.
15979 L.-Cpl. Arthur, Charles F.
15980 Pte. M'Ilwraith, James.
15981 L.-Sergt. Pooley, R.S.
15982 Pte. Campbell, Samuel.
15983 Pte. M'Allan, John T.
15984 Sergt. Lugton, G.D.
15985 Pte. M'Walter, Thomas Scott.
15986 Pte. Wood, John.
15987 L.-Cpl. Mackie, William R.N.
15988 Pte. Pooley, Francis H.
15989 Sig.-Sergt. Marshall, John H.
15990 Pte. Pollock, James Watson.
15991 Pte. MacKinnon, Robert A.
15992 Pte. Reid, James William M.

15993 Pte. Scott, James.
15994 Pte. M'Veigh, Hugh.
15095 Pte. Gregor, William.
15996 Pte. Salmine, John.
15997 Pte. Forsyth, Stewart.
15998 Cpl. Walker, Robert.
15999 Pte. M'Kenzie, John M.
16000 Pte. Crosbie, Robert.
16001 Pte. Boyd, William.
16002 Pte. Main, John.
16003 Pte. Cattell, Joseph.
16004 Pte. Deans, John K.
16005 Pte. Watt, Thomas S.
16006 Pte. Kerr, John.
16007 Pte. M'Lean, Norman.
16008 Pte. Wood, David S.
16009 L.-Cpl. Main, Samuel Hope.
16010 Pte. M'Lintock, William.
16011 Cpl. Brodie, James L.
16012 Pte. Mason, George Bishop.
16013 Pte. Mullan, William John
16014 Pte. M'Donald, Robert Barr.
16015 L.-Cpl. Turnbull, David.
16016 Pte. Abrahamson, A.
16017 Pte. Brownlee, George.
16018 Pte. Hood, Robert.
16019 Sergt. Wattie, Alex.
16020 Sergt. Lee, Edward.
16021 Pte. Kirk, Robert.
16022 Pte. Cassels, Hugh L.
16023 Pte. Maclagan, Douglas.
16024 L.-Cpl. M'Allister, John.
16025 L.-Cpl. Longmuir, Robert.
16026 Pte. Keir, John A.L.
16027 Pte. Blair, Fred.
16028 Pte. Gemmell, Alex.
16029 Pte. Nixon, David.
16030 Pte. Ritchie, William.
16031 Pte. Dick, Andrew.
16032 Pte. Kinnear, Ian F.G.

16033 Pte. Morton, Alfred.
16034 L.-Cpl. Paton, John.
16035 Pte. Tait, William.
16036 Pte. Ferguson, James.
16037 Pte. Miller, Thomas.
16038 Pte. Friend, Joseph.
16039 Pte. Muirhead, John.
16040 Pte. Young, George Graham.
16041 Pte. Langlands, John F.
16042 Pte. Lovat, M.
16043 Cpl. Smith, A. W.
16044 Pte. Harvey, Kenneth R.
16045 Pte. Boyd, William.
16046 Pte. Boyd, John.
16047 Pte. Ramsay, George.
16048 Pte. Morton, Thomas.
16049 Pte. Johnston, James K.
16050 L.-Cpl. Pickles, Frank.
16051 Pte. Jackson, James.
16052 Pte. Dalziel, William.
16053 Cpl. Todd, James C.
16054 Pte. Millar, John.
16055 Pte. Cunningham, John.
16056 L.-Cpl. Drennan, Andrew Adam.
16057 Pte. Thomson, James M'K.
16058 Sergt. Paterson, Walter A.
16059 Pte. Ness, George.
16060 Pte. Barrett, F.G.
16061 Pte. Spiers, Alex. R.
16062 Pte. Tait, William.
16063 Pte. Anderson, Charles.
16064 Pte. Hutton, James.
16065 Pte. McLaughlin, William.
16066 Pte. Higgins, Robert K.
16067 Pte. M'Kenzie, Duncan M'R.
16068 Pte. M'Lellan, John.
16069 Pte. M'Rorie, William D.
16070 Pte. Dickson, William.
16071 Pte. Miller, James.
16072 L.-Cpl. Martin, George F.

16073 Pte. Gardiner, Alex.
16074 Pte. White, William Thomson.
16075 Pte. Wood, Joe.
16076 Pte. Wallace, Thomas.
16077 Pte. M'Kenzie, Thomas D.
16078 Pte. Adam, Andrew Ralston.
16079 Pte. Kelly, James H.
16080 Pte. Dunsmore, Thomas S.
16081 Pte. Cameron, Arthur.
16082 Pte. Lavelle, James.
16083 Pte. Martin, Hugh Albert.
16084 Sergt. Gilbert, Young.
16085 Pte. Parker, William.
16086 Pte. M'Ewan, Thomas W.
16087 Pte. Fraser, William.
16088 Pte. Rae, David.
16089 Pte. Reid, David Boyd.
16090 Pte. Scott, Alex.
16091 Pte. Watt, William.
16092 Pte. Hutchison, William.
16093 Cpl. Thomson, William.
16094 Pte. Findlay, John Walter.
16095 Pte. Ross, John M.
16096 Pte. Wright, William.
16097 Pte. Allan, James.
16098 Pte. Relton, Arthur N.
16099 Pte. Adamson, Joseph.
16100 Cpl. Dickson, John.
16101 Pte. Clark, G. M'I.
16102 Pte. Struthers, William.
16103 Pte. Campbell, Stuart.
16104 Pte. Cruickshank, J.C.
16105 Pte. Johnstone, George.
16106 Pte. Williamson, Andrew.
16107 Pte. M'Intyre, James.
16108 Pte. Grindlay, Charles Percy.
16109 Pte. Wallace, William.
16110 Pte. Boyd, John Shaw.
16111 Pte. Campbell, John.
16112 Pte. Mathieson, Stanley.

16113 Pte. M'Pherson, George L.
16114 Pte. Kennedy, David.
16115 Pte. Robertson, H.
16116 Pte. Grierson, William Ian.
16117 Pte. Rooney, Alex.
16118 Pte. Fairfax, G.A.F.
16119 Pte. Chalmers, Thomas.
16120 Pte. Maxwell, Robert.
16121 Pte. Beveridge, Erskine W.
16122 Pte. Napier, John.
16123 Sergt. Johnstone, S.
16124 Pte. Kilcullen, Thomas.
16125 Pte. Muil, Frank.
16126 Pte. Napier, William.
16127 Pte. M'Master, Alex.
16128 Pte. Gibson, Thomas Bell.
16129 Pte. Gregory, William.
16130 Pte. Brunsdon, Henry George.
16131 Pte. M'Gartland, Patrick.
16132 Sergt. Beck, Andrew.
16133 Pte. Tod, Frederick M.C.
16134 Pte. Dunlop, William.
16135 Pte. Kelly, Charles.
16136 Pte. Kennedy, John.
16137 Pte. Nicoll, George L.
16138 Pte. Toole, James L.
16139 L.-Sergt. Watson, Peter D.
16140 Pte. M'Intyre, Archibald.
16141 Pte. Graham, A.W.B.
16142 Pte. Stubbs, James F.
16143 Pte. Niven, John L.L.
16144 Pte. Simpson, Donald.
16145 Pte. M'Innes, Archibald C.
16146 Pte. Milligan, Robert.
16147 Pte. Williamson, Charles.
16148 Pte. Mackay, Angus.
16149 L.-Cpl. Thorburn, Henry.
16150 Pte. Morrison, Charles H.
16151 Pte. Archibald, Andrew.
16152 Pte. Campbell, Andrew.

16153 Pte. Morgan, John S.
16154 Pte. Grassick, Henry J.
16155 Pte. Campbell, William.
16156 L.-Cpl. M'Callum, Herbert L.
16157 Pte. Ewing, John.
16158 Pte. M'Lean, Angus.
16159 Pte. Graham, W.F.
16160 Pte. Hamilton, J.
16161 Pte. Black, David S.
16162 Pte. Cousland, Archibald.
16163 Pte. Dunlop, Colin B.
16164 Pte. Drew, George Millar.
16165 Pte. Fotheringham, James R.
16166 Pte. Kerr, John Galloway.
16167 Pte. Oswald, Robert R.
16168 L.-Cpl. Racionzer, J.L.
16169 Pte. Sinclair, John F.
16170 Pte. Black, Thomas.
16171 Pte. Paterson, David.
16172 Pte. Wilson, W.R.
16173 Pte. Kay, James J.
16174 L.-Cpl. Munro, Ronald.
16175 Pte. Liston, John.
16176 Pte. Paton, Robert.
16177 L.-Cpl. Spence, John George.
16178 Pte. Thomson, Ernest.
16179 Cpl. Barrie, Alex.
16180 Pte. Aitken, Robert.
16181 Pte. Dewar, J.F.
16182 Pte. Henderson, Hugh.
16183 Pte. Lane, Andrew.
16184 Pte. M'Dougall, David.
16185 Pte. Deacon, R.E.
16186 Pte. Stroud, Archibald William.
16187 Pte. Brown, Archibald.
16188 Pte. Manson, William.
16189 L.-Sergt. Robertson, Alexander Y.
16190 Pte. Gauld, Andrew.
16191 Pte. Imrie, William.
16192 Pte. M'Killop, Hugh.

16193 Pte. Porter, John.
16194 Pte. Sanderson, John T.
16195 Cpl. Andrews, John.
16196 Pte. Smith, James.
16197 Pte. Waters, Robert R.
16198 Pte. Watson, William.
16199 Pte. Davies, Howard L.
16200 Pte. Thomson, George.
16201 L.-Cpl. Whiteford, Thomas R.
16202 Pte. Aitken, Thomas.
16203 Pte. Wood, Alex.
16204 L.-Cpl. Law, Robert.
16205 Pte. Thomson, John.
16206 Pte. Park, R.
16207 Pte. Ferguson, Robert.
16208 Pte. Hutcheson, William J.F.
16209 Pte. Gardner, H.A.
16210 Pte. Robertson, W.B.
16211 Pte. Walker, Arthur P.
16212 Pte. Miller, Alex. S.
16213 Pte. Scott, Charles R.G.
16214 L.-Cpl. Kemp, Archibald J.
16215 Pte. Ewing, George H.
16216 Pte. Harper, Alex. C.
16217 Pte. Henderson, James.
16218 Pte. Hill, Archibald.
16219 Pte. Dempster, G.C.
16220 Pte. Taylor, Matthew.
16221 Pte. Adam, John L.
16222 Pte. Biggart, John.
16223 Pte. M'Leod, Angus.
16224 Pte. Reid, Archibald M.
16225 Pte. Allan, Hugh Robert.
16226 Pte. Crowley, John.
16227 Pte. Hawthorn, Charles.
16228 Pte. Miller, William.
16229 Pte. Herring, Frank M.
16230 L.-Cpl. Barrie, George Alston.
16231 Pte. Struth, James S.
16232 Pte. Ward, William Allan.

16233 Pte. Ross, David.
16234 Pte. Walker, Roderick.
16235 Pte. Carmichael, Duncan.
16236 Pte. Hamilton, Arthur.
16237 Pte. Dodds, James.
16238 Pte. M'Millan, John A.
16239 Pte. Fearby, John E.
16240 L.-Cpl. Okell, Cyril.
16241 Pte. Mathieson, Alex.
16242 Pte. M'Ewan, Malcolm W.
16243 L.-Cpl. Mair, William Craig.
16244 L.-Cpl. Macdonald, John.
16245 Pte. Dickie, William.
16246 Pte. Hyslop, John.
16247 Pte. Miller, Kenneth S.
16248 Pte. Laing, John.
16249 Pte. Watt, Edwin.
16250 Pte. Levey, Jack.
16251 Pte. Carmichael, Archibald.
16252 Pte. Cree, Walter Hill.
16253 Pte. Bennett, David.
16254 Pte. Coats, Thomas.
16255 Pte. Thomson, Robert W.
16256 Pte. Mitchell, C.H.
16257 Pte. Powell, James E.L.
16258 Pte. Andrew, John.
16259 Pte. Mowat, Alex.
16260 Pte. Gardner, James.
16261 Pte. Thistle, Robert James.
16262 Pte. Macaulay, William.
16263 Pte. Gemmell, Allan.
16264 Pte. Miller, John F.
16265 L.-Cpl. Hall, Robert.
16266 Pte. M'Queen, John Duff.
16267 Pte. Aird, Allan Muir.
16268 Pte. Hayes, John T.
16269 Pte. Stewart, C. Campbell.
16270 Pte. Campbell, Jack M'N.
16271 Pte. M'Nair, Thomas.
16272 Pte. Chisholm, Alex.

16273 Pte. Robertson, William P.
16274 L.-Cpl. Anderson, John S.
16275 Pte. Russell, Hugh Ramsay.
16276 Pte. Carmichael, Hugh H.
16277 L.-Cpl. Neary, Thomas.
16278 Pte. Thomson, Adam John.
16279 Pte. King, John W.
16280 Pte. Neilson, George.
16281 Pte. Simpson, John[128]
16282 Pte. Barbour, James.
16283 Pte. Anderson, John.
16284 Pte. Peters, David.
16285 Pte. Jamieson, George William.
16286 Pte. Wilson, Thomas.
16287 Pte. Morrison, Adam C.
16288 Pte. Kerr, John.
16289 Pte. Anderson, James.
16290 Pte. Wilson, John.
16291 Pte. Laird, William.
16292 Pte. Parker, William.
16293 Pte. Murray, William.
16294 Pte. Andrew, Donald.
16295 Pte. Glover, Victor.
16296 Pte. Armour, Andrew.
16297 Pte. M'Dowell, John.
16298 Pte. Caldwell, Richard T.
16299 Pte. Smith, William.
 2684 Pte. Simpson, George P.
 2685 Pte. Robertson, David M.
 2686 Pte. Harris, Ernest.
 2687 Pte. Burleigh, F.S.
 2688 Pte. Watson, Joseph.
 2689 Pte. Sinclair, George.
 2690 Pte. Watson, Stanley M.W.
 2691 Pte. Miller, James.
 2692 Pte. Nicol, William Kerr.
 2693 Pte. King, William.
 2694 Pte. M'Culloch, Walter.
 2695 Pte. Park, Matthew.
 2696 Pte. Murdoch, James.

2697 Pte. Laverty, Henry.
2698 Pte. Jordan, Harold W.
2699 Pte. Johnston, James
2700 Pte. Swan, James.
2701 Pte. Colvil, Harold C.
2702 Pte. Hendry, H.G.
2703 Pte. Heaverman, Walter E.
2704 Pte. Yates, Robert.
2705 Pte. Whytock, James.
2706 L.-Cpl. M'Munn, James.
2707 Pte. M'Knight, James.
2708 Pte. Carswell, James.
2709 Pte. Sinclair, George.
2710 Pte. Taylor, Hugh B.
2711 Pte. Bennet, James.
2712 Pte. Laing, Robert M'L.
2713 Pte. Johnston, William E.
2714 L.-Cpl. Gilchrist, James.
2715 Pte. Scott, H. Fred.
2716 Pte. Neish, Alexander M.
2717 Pte. Robertson, James C.
2718 Pte. Gilmour, Murray.
2719 Pte. M'Innes, Duncan.
2720 Pte. M'Kinnon, Robert B.
2721 L.-Cpl. Craig, Robert.
2722 Pte. Hutton, George L.
2723 Pte. Montgomery, Andrew D.
2724 Pte. Killin, William.
2725 Pte. Ramage, John.
2726 L.-Cpl. Henderson, James G.
2727 Pte. Glennie, William.
2728 Pte. Mackie, John B.
2729 Pte. Gemmell, Charles S.
2730 Pte. Herbert, Robert.
2731 Pte. Niven, A.C.L.
2732 Pte. Brown, A.G.
2733 Pte. Paterson, William.
2734 Pte. Young, James.
2735 Pte. Young, Robert.
2736 Pte. Scott, Robert.

2737 Pte. Stewart, Daniel.
2738 Pte. Preston, James.
2739 L.-Cpl. Lindsay, Matthew.
2740 Pte. Finlay, James G.
2741 Pte. Mitchell, Robert C.
2742 Pte. Taylor, John.
2743 Pte. M'Ilvaney, James.
2744 Pte. Hunter, John C.
2745 Pte. Grant, Douglas.
2746 Pte. Smith, D.F.
2749 Pte. Fulton, Archibald H.
2750 Pte. Garner, Robt. K.
2751 Pte. Grant, Alastair M.
2752 Pte. Howieson, Peter.
2753 Pte. Kidd, Thomas B.
2754 Pte. Lochhead, James.
2755 Pte. Ovenstone, James.
2756 Pte. Owen, George.
2757 Pte. Russell, George.
2758 C.Q.M.S. Scott, William.
2759 Pte. Smith, Ernest M.
2760 Pte. Wright, John.
2761 Pte. Jaffrey, William.
2762 Pte. Hardie, John.
2763 Pte. Tennant, Archibald A.
2764 Pte. O'Beirne, Thomas.
2765 Pte. Wilkie, Robert James D.
2766 Pte. Goodfellow, James.
2767 Pte. Bain, Bruce.
2768 Pte. Blakely, John.
2769 Pte. Millar, H.S.M.
2770 Pte. Wright, William.
2771 Pte. Waddell, John.
2772 Pte. Gemmell, Hugh K.
2773 Pte. M'Creath, David.
2774 Pte. Forsyth, George S.
2775 Pte. Stewart, Donald.
2776 Pte. Mackie, James.
2777 Pte. Hamilton, Andrew.
2778 Pte. M'Farlane, William.

2779 Pte. Currie, James.
2780 Pte. Craig, Thomas L.M.
2781 Pte. M'Nidder, Alex. M.
2782 Pte. Ward, James M.
2783 Pte. Hamilton, James M.
2784 Pte. Ross, Alex. M'K.
2785 Pte. Murphy, Albert E.
2786 Pte. Clark, John.
2787 Pte. Sanderson, Thomas.
2788 Pte. Grierson, William.
2789 Pte. Crawford, David.
2790 Pte. Smith, Hugh M'F.
2791 Pte. Askham, S.G.
2792 Pte. Stevenson, John.
2793 Pte. Pettigrew, William.
2794 Pte. Pettigrew, Thomas T.
2795 Pte. Yuill, William T.L.
2796 Pte. Muir, James Craig.
2797 Pte. Leiper, Frank.
2798 Pte. Liddell, Robert.
2799 Pte. Allwart, John Charles.
2800 Pte. Gilhooly, Michael.
2801 Pte. M'Donald, James.
2802 Pte. Rose, Arthur O.
2803 Pte. Stevenson, Colin Campbell.
2804 Pte. M'Farlane, William C.
2805 Pte. M'Williams, Bertram.
2806 Pte. Cameron, William S.
2807 Pte. Dale, Robert.
2808 Pte. Irving, Charles.
2809 Pte. Blythe, Roland F.
2810 Pte. Shearer, R.W.
2811 Pte. Holmes, W.
2812 Pte. Bryson, Matthew.
2813 Pte. Taylor, Archibald A.
2814 Pte. Gray, Edwin.
2815 Pte. Bryden, David.
2816 Pte. Stevenson, John.
2817 Pte. Catchpool, Albert.
2818 Pte. Baird, Arthur J.

2819 Pte. M'Kechnie, John.
2820 Pte. Napier, Claud H.
2821 Pte. M'Lachlan, Fred. E.
2822 Pte. Harris, John L.H.
2823 Pte. Adams, Andrew.
2824 Pte. Torrance, James.
2825 Pte. Murray, Edward.
2826 Pte. Bain, Charles.
2827 Pte. Hourston, David William.
2828 Pte. Lee, George.
2829 Pte. Mackenzie, James E.
2830 Pte. Stoddart, Adam.
2831 Pte. M'Callum, James.
2832 Pte. Wylie, William.
2833 Pte. Watson, James F.
2834 Pte. M'Phee, James.
2835 Pte. Kennedy, James D.
2836 Pte. Davidson, Charles.
2837 Pte. Hogg, H.
2838 Pte. Robb, William.
2839 Pte. Ferguson, George S.
2840 Pte. M'Intyre, James L.
2841 Pte. Morrison, John.
2842 Pte. M'Vicar, Alex.
2843 Pte. Jack, James L.
2844 Pte. Adams, George Ross.
2845 Pte. Wilson, Frank.
2846 Pte. Broadfoot, J.R.
2847 Pte. Miller, James.
2848 Pte. Murdoch, Henry.
2849 Pte. MacWilliams, James.
2850 Pte. Wilkie, A.K.
2851 Pte. Falconer, John.
2852 Pte. M'Murdo, Jack.
2853 Pte. Ramsay, Robert B.
2854 Pte. Copland, Lawrence.
2855 Pte. Monoghan, William.
2856 Pte. Reid, John H.
2857 Pte. Cowie, Robert.
2858 Pte. Halloran, William.

2859 Pte. Clark, Noel M.
2860 Pte. M'Kinlay, William.
2861 Pte. M'Intyre, Hugh.
2862 Pte. Howie, John Brown.
2863 Pte. Coupar, Arthur.
2864 Pte. Wilson, Thomas Jackson.
2865 Pte. Kerr, John Rennie.
2866 Pte. Sleater, William.
2867 Pte. Morton, John Craig.
2868 Pte. Constable, James.
2869 Pte. Melville, William.
2870 Pte. Oliver, John.
2871 Pte. Dunlop, Richard O.G.
2872 Pte. M'Jannet, John C.
2873 Pte. Hervey, Robert.
2874 Pte. Tindal, David.
2875 Pte. Wileman, Robert.
2876 Pte. Hamilton, James I.
2877 Pte. Watson, Duncan Roy.
2878 Pte. Nicol, Thomas.
2879 Pte. Hastings, S.
2880 Pte. Smith, G.M.
2881 Pte. Sloan, D.
2882 Pte. Farquhar, John F.
2883 Pte. Paterson, Charles.
2884 Pte. Wilson, James.
2885 Pte. Garrioch, Robert.
2886 Pte. Wooley, Archibald K.
2887 Pte. Black, James M'K.
2888 Pte. Ingram, James.
2889 Pte. Craig, George.
2890 Pte. Cunningham, Andrew.
2891 Pte. Cameron, Lachlan A.
2892 Pte. Gillies, Henry.
2893 Pte. Peacock, David Kerr.
2894 Pte. M'Donald, Robert.
2895 Pte. Henderson, George.
2896 L.-Cpl. Scott, James.
2897 Pte. Dinwoodie, William.
2898 Pte. Birrell, Robert.

2899 Pte. M'Kerrow, G.
2900 Pte. Miller, John G.
2901 Pte. Foote, George Alex.
2902 Pte. Stewart, Thomas.
2903 Pte. Murray, John K.
2904 Pte. Steele, George James.
2905 Pte. Dietrich, William J.L.
2906 Pte. Miller, Duncan.
2907 Pte. Ramsay, John.
2908 Pte. Struthers, David W.
2909 Pte. Conway, Frank Joseph.
2910 Pte. Lang, Archibald.
2911 Pte. Watson, Donald Grassick.
2912 Pte. Evans, Joseph Howard.
2913 Pte. Burt, Henry.
2914 Pte. Dykes, James A.
2915 Pte. Kirkwood, Alexander.
2916 Pte. Young, John Douglas.
2917 Pte. Calder, James Barclay.
2918 Pte. Orr, William.
2919 Pte. Park, Thomas W.U.
2920 Pte. Bennie, Hugh O.
2921 Pte. Allan, William.
2922 Pte. Haft, Saul.
2923 Pte. Rosenbloom, Harry.
2924 Pte. Brown, William Robert.
2925 Pte. Linton, William F.
2926 Pte. Burns, Robert.
2927 Pte. Munn, Douglas.
2928 Pte. Macpherson, Donald B.
2929 Pte. M'Gugan, John.
2930 Pte. M'Innes, James.
2931 Pte. Colliston, James.
2932 Pte. Alston, Thomas.
2933 Pte. Adam, William.
2934 Pte. Green, Alfred.
2935 Pte. Lauder, Alex. Duncan.
2936 Pte. Angus, Thomas.
2937 Pte. Dewar, Robert Nisbet.
2938 Pte. M'Lean, Murdoch.

2939 Pte. Preston, James D.
2940 Pte. Young, George.
2941 Pte. Sherry, John.
2942 Pte. Bryce, Allan.
2943 Pte. M'Millan, John R.
2944 Pte. Robertson, John.
2945 Pte. Graham, James.
2946 Pte. Neasham, Robert.
2947 Pte. Shaw, James.
2948 Pte. M'Donald, Alex.
2949 Pte. M'Naught, Alex.
2950 Pte. Cross, Robert M'K.
2951 Pte. Doig, Thomas F.
2952 Pte. Howie, John.
2953 Pte. M'Kenzie, Duncan William.
2954 Pte. Stephenson, Fred.
2955 Pte. Barker, George Charles.
2956 Pte. Garvie, Ernest L.
2957 Pte. Hutchison, E. Deans.
2958 Pte. Harrower, Alex.
2959 Pte. Baird, James H.H.
2960 Pte. Ross, Thomas.
2961 Pte. Watson, Thomas H.
2962 Pte. Skinner, John.
2963 Pte. Begg, Robert Craig.
2964 Pte. Buchan, Bertram Gray.
2965 Pte. Carlson, Edward P.
2966 Pte. Hastie, Robert L.
2967 Pte. Fulton, Matthews.
2968 Pte. Watson, T. Greig.
2969 Pte. Allan, Joseph D.
2970 Pte. Miller, John.
2971 Pte. Kerr, Donald.
2972 Pte. Barr, Matthew.
2973 Pte. Thompson, Alfred W.
2974 Pte. Gibson, Arthur Charles.
2975 Pte. Sorrie, George.
2976 Pte. Hamilton, Charles.
2977 Pte. Gauld, Hector L.
2978 Pte. Holmes, James Y.

2979 Pte. Winning, Isaac.
2980 Pte. Raffles, Alex.
2981 Pte. Thomson, Thomas Craig.
2982 Pte. Boyle, John.
2983 Pte. M'Naught, William.
2984 Pte. Scott, Thomas H.C.
2985 Pte. Garmory, Thomas.
2986 Pte. Mitchell, John.
2987 Pte. Scott, Thomas.
2988 Pte. Brown, Thomas Montgomery.
2989 Pte. Fleming, Alex.
2990 Pte. Fawcett, Cyril John.
2991 Pte. Grant, William N.
2992 Pte. Irving, Alex.
2993 Pte. M'Greehin, Frederick J.
2994 Pte. Sawers, William Brown.
2995 Pte. Ireland, William B.B.
2996 Pte. Dow, Hugh Auskin.
2997 Pte. Connar, Norman.
2998 Pte. Baxter, William.
23001 Pte. Baxter, Thomas.
23002 Pte. Morton, George.
23003 Pte. Bruce, William C.
23004 Pte. Banks, William Stephen.
23005 Pte. Peat, Harold Ross.
23006 Pte. M'Queen, James.
23007 Pte. Black, Max.
23008 Pte. Robertson, James.
23009 Pte. Campbell, Roland.
23010 Pte. Bell, James.
23011 Pte. Drummond, Alex. G.
23012 Pte. Kerr, William.
23013 Pte. M'Clymont, Robert.
23014 Pte. Brown, Hector M'D.
23015 Pte. Meadows, Bentley.
23016 Pte. Train, Thomas.
23017 Pte. Sutherland, Daniel.
23018 Pte. Watt, John.
23019 Pte. Halliday, William.
23020 Pte. M'Cormack, John Jeffrey.

23021 Pte. Gray, John.
23022 Pte. Dickson, John.
23023 Pte. Anderson, William S.
23024 Pte. M'Gowan, Archibald James.
23025 Pte. Farquhar, Henry Steven.
23026 Pte. Somerville, Peter.
23027 Pte. MacIntyre, William M.
23028 Pte. Spence, Ernest Alex.
23029 Pte. Ross, E.N.
23030 Pte. Drummond, J.
23031 Pte. Dick, James.
23032 Pte. Ogilvie, James.
23033 Pte. Johnston, John.
23034 Pte. Monteath, William.
23035 Pte. Kirkhope, James B.

LEONAUR

ALSO FROM LEONAUR

AVAILABLE IN SOFTCOVER OR HARDCOVER WITH DUST JACKET

THE 9TH—THE KING'S (LIVERPOOL REGIMENT) IN THE GREAT WAR 1914 - 1918 *by Enos H. G. Roberts*—Mersey to mud—war and Liverpool men.

THE GAMBARDIER *by Mark Severn*—The experiences of a battery of Heavy artillery on the Western Front during the First World War.

FROM MESSINES TO THIRD YPRES *by Thomas Floyd*—A personal account of the First World War on the Western front by a 2/5th Lancashire Fusilier.

THE IRISH GUARDS IN THE GREAT WAR - VOLUME 1 *by Rudyard Kipling*—Edited and Compiled from Their Diaries and Papers—The First Battalion.

THE IRISH GUARDS IN THE GREAT WAR - VOLUME 1 *by Rudyard Kipling*—Edited and Compiled from Their Diaries and Papers—The Second Battalion.

ARMOURED CARS IN EDEN *by K. Roosevelt*—An American President's son serving in Rolls Royce armoured cars with the British in Mesopatamia & with the American Artillery in France during the First World War.

CHASSEUR OF 1914 *by Marcel Dupont*—Experiences of the twilight of the French Light Cavalry by a young officer during the early battles of the great war in Europe.

TROOP HORSE & TRENCH *by R.A. Lloyd*—The experiences of a British Lifeguardsman of the household cavalry fighting on the western front during the First World War 1914-18.

THE EAST AFRICAN MOUNTED RIFLES *by C.J. Wilson*—Experiences of the campaign in the East African bush during the First World War.

THE LONG PATROL *by George Berrie*—A Novel of Light Horsemen from Gallipoli to the Palestine campaign of the First World War.

THE FIGHTING CAMELIERS *by Frank Reid*—The exploits of the Imperial Camel Corps in the desert and Palestine campaigns of the First World War.

STEEL CHARIOTS IN THE DESERT *by S. C. Rolls*—The first world war experiences of a Rolls Royce armoured car driver with the Duke of Westminster in Libya and in Arabia with T.E. Lawrence.

WITH THE IMPERIAL CAMEL CORPS IN THE GREAT WAR *by Geoffrey Inchbald*—The story of a serving officer with the British 2nd battalion against the Senussi and during the Palestine campaign.